TEN THINGS EVERY FOSTER CHILD WISHES YOU KNEW

TEN THINGS EVERY FOSTER CHILD WISHES YOU KNEW

ROWAN ADERYN

To my girls, who have taught me that happy endings are ours to write. Your joy and love inspire me every day to be a better parent. Thank you for always sharing this journey with me.

To Stephen, who not only rescued me from a world I longed to escape but continually supports every dream and pursuit. Thank you for dancing with me in the rain.

To the care community, whose strength and perseverance inspire me daily. Your dedication to a better future is my greatest motivation.

To the incredible individuals working tirelessly to support us—foster parents, social workers, support workers, and charity leaders. Futures like mine would not be possible without your hard work and commitment. Special thanks to Sarah Jacoby for her invaluable guidance on Ten Things.

And to everyone reading Ten Things Every Foster Child Wishes You Knew—thank you for your willingness to learn, understand, and shine a light on the children who need us most.

CONTENTS

Introduction

When I was a child, I loved nothing more than playing in the road with the other children in our street, each shouting "Car" at the top of our lungs and retreating to the pavement in a flash when a vehicle interrupted our game. Or neatly sitting my dolls in a row whilst I taught them maths or read them a story. My favourite place in the world was my 'TTT' (Take That Tunnel), a small, long space in my bedroom which led to a tiny window overlooking the city. I had plastered the walls and ceiling in every Take That poster I could find and would often lie on the floor surrounded by their pictures, singing their songs aloud.

Behind those moments of childhood bliss there was a dark reality which engulfed most of my days. I remember the first time I found the bathroom covered in blood, my red footprints leaving a trail behind me as I fearfully retreated to my room. I remember the shouting voices as they echoed up four flights of stairs. I remember no one being there when I got home from school and trying my best to make beans and toast for my little sister. I remember the feeling of hands around my neck or later in life touching me as my skin crawled, stomach turned, and an icy fire burnt throughout my body. Those moments forcing me to seek out any whisper of hope, any crack of light in a world consumed by abuse and fear.

When I was ten years old it was apparent to the local social services that we were not safe or being cared for in the way we should. My little sister and I were taken into care. My world however traumatic was thrown further into uncertainty before finding a more settled ground. For the next four years I spent my time in the care of one foster family. I still had supervised contact with my mother, being escorted by medical professionals and social workers through locked doors into staged family rooms where we would sit and try to cram a lifetime into an hour. Every couple of weeks we would spend time at my father's house. It was there I was allowed to smoke and drink and essentially run riot. Everyone around us applied huge amounts of effort to maintain those two-family connections, not seeing the damage which was being done.

These years of shared care were the quiet before and after the storm. When I left care to return full time to my father the abuse I experienced increased exponentially, until I escaped in my early twenties. But this book is not the story of my life. This book is inspired by the hundreds of conversations with people supporting those in care. For all the wonderful foster parents present, past and future. For the social workers and support workers. For the individuals who support our most vulnerable children. For those who want to understand how they can help. Offered in the hope it can answer some of the questions they hold, and shape the thinking which will allow us to improve the future of all children in care.

Over one hundred thousand vulnerable children in the UK currently rely on the care system for their safety and wellbeing. These numbers do not include children placed with relatives through kinship care. These children have often experienced abuse, neglect or other forms of hardship, leaving them with emotional and developmental challenges, creating barriers and disadvantages which impact them throughout their lives.

It is a heartbreaking reality that for most of the children who grow up in care their futures are a fait accompli. They are resigned to a life of poor health, educational, housing and employment outcomes. They are more likely to experience homelessness than go to university, with care experienced people making up a quarter of the population of individuals experiencing homelessness. They are seventy per cent more likely to die prematurely and if they do make it into employment, experience one of the biggest pay gaps in the UK.

I was lucky to avoid many of the horrific outcomes care experienced people face. I have two of the most amazing children in the world, have been happily married for over sixteen years. I have been hugely successful in my career, and I even went to university eventually. I have enjoyed so many aspects of life most care experienced people never get to know.

Throughout this book I touch on moments of my journey and the journeys of those I have known in the hope that these examples offer you a window into the perspective of those children we care for. Children who have known chaos, rejection and fear on a level many of us will thankfully never know. You can dip in and out, take the parts which resonate and leave the rest behind. These are my words and experiences alone. I cannot speak for all children in care. I am not trying to write a research paper or psychological guide. There are far better people in the world for that task. Some of what I write may have a grounding in research. Much of what follows is simply the outcome of walking this path, constantly reflecting, a thirst to understand why, and my own desire to be a good parent.

The thinking which follows should never replace great training, lessons learnt or the variety of policies which may be in place to protect the children you care for. The ideas are intended to spark a thought or ignite a conversation. All of which should be considered within the context of what is best for any individual living in the care world.

My greatest hope is that we can build a future where every child in care, regardless of their background, has the chance to experience the love, support and opportunities that led me to where I am today. That we can recognise the skills, value and thinking care experienced people bring to our communities and workplaces. That we can establish support and approaches which nurture and heal, allowing them to achieve their full potential. For those children and all those who come after us here are the ten things I wish my foster parents and those caring for me knew.

I Need Boundaries, But I Don't Understand the Rules

When I found myself deposited in a stranger's home to live, I quickly became aware of how little I knew. The first day I arrived, I sat almost frozen on a kitchen chair for hours. Not aware where I could and couldn't go, what I should or shouldn't say. I silently observed as my foster mother pottered around the place unpacking shopping and making cakes and tea. It was the quietest I ever remember being in my life. I don't think I even knew the questions to ask to help me navigate my newfound environment. All I could do was sit and wait for those unspoken rules to become clear.

We all learn a certain set of unspoken rules. Anything from do you brush your teeth before or after breakfast, should I flush the toilet if I use it in the night, can I watch the television whenever I like or are there certain times of the day, should I clear my plate of food, am I expected to clear the table, do you wear socks with sandals, am I allowed to wind down the window in the car. There are hundreds of these rules we each operate under without really noticing every single day.

Over the years those rules slowly and surely became obvious. I learnt that the television downstairs was for the children. I learnt that if you didn't wash regularly, you were at risk of being thrown in the shower with your clothes on. To always leave the remote control on the left-hand side of the sofa. To not wear makeup. To keep your room tidy. To leave your shoes by the door. The list was endless.

There are all sorts of unspoken rules we establish in our homes. Helping a child who is new to your home understand these unspoken rules will help them to feel more comfortable and build a solid foundation of communication. Before tackling this task with a child, it is valuable to firstly reflect on what types of unwritten rules may exist in your life. Here are some areas to consider.

1.1 The Language of Unwritten Rules

Emotional Expressions Most of us develop social norms of what the preferred emotional communication is within a home. Within any home we can vary from a subtle "chin up" attitude, to a more extreme "don't cry or I will give you something to cry about". In my first home I learnt to hide all emotion. Any emotion was dangerous. A happy joyous emotion could trigger my mother. Her mental illness created a muddled sense of guilt and pain when others experienced joy. Whilst sadness or heaven forbid anger would trigger my father and lead to verbal or physical violence. Reflecting on the emotional vibe within your home can help you establish where a child's behaviour may feel extreme if at odds with this.

Conflict and Communication This can range from a very direct matter of fact form of communication to a more indirect informal discussion. If someone else has done something wrong, or if I have done something, how this is communicated and who I should tell can vary massively. Is your home very structured with family meetings and times to connect? Or do you prefer to deal with things as they arise and off the cuff. For many children the way they will have been taught to communicate will not have been a choice, but essential to surviving the environment they were in.

Gender Roles and Responsibilities More common in some households than others, anything from simple tasks like cooking and cleaning, to the games you can play or the things you can wear, may vary hugely. This distinction or lack of distinction in roles may be confusing for a child if they have experienced a difference in this space before. That confusion can cause further discomfort and worry as the lack of consistency challenges their understanding.

Behavioural Expectations These might include anything from the volume with which a child should speak, to the way the door or the phone should be answered. The standards around how much independence is encouraged, or obedience valued. Can a child be inquisitive and ask what you are doing when you are working, or should you be left in peace to concentrate?

Personal Achievement and Validation Should a child share their successes or is this considered bragging. Do you value performance in school, sporting ability or artistic flair. The child may have been raised with a totally different set of expectations and find themselves going from a position of respect and validation to a position of diminished worth. Recognising where you place value and the bias to consider certain things better will allow you to understand when to approach rules with rigidity or flexibility. We often enforce firmer rules on the things we hold with greater value.

Resource Management and Financial Control Will the child be given an allowance or pocket money for chores. Are they allowed to use any of the toiletries in the bathroom, can they eat what food they like, or are they restricted in what they can take. Unwritten rules around resource allocation are important to ensure basic needs are comfortably met.

Many children in the care system will experience multiple placements, all with different unwritten rules. Every time they are introduced to a new home, relationship or environment they are expected to relearn these rules. This can cause confusion and frustration for all those involved. Even where placements are stable the amount of changing key relationships for a child in care can create a need to be constantly relearning rules of engagement. Be patient and consider ways to support them in building their understanding.

1.2 A Guide to the Home

One way to try to support children in understanding the expectations placed on them is to sit down together and create a house manual. This can be very visual or descriptive depending on the age and needs of the child. It is important to do this in an open and collaborative way. To sit together and discuss the things they would like to know and the things you would help them to understand. It is important to ensure they feel their voice is heard in this process. A great starting point can be to ask them first what they would like included. Topics may incorporate:

Daily Routines:

- Wake-up/bed time: Setting consistent times with some flexibility.
- Chores: Assign age-appropriate chores and create a schedule.
- Meals and snacks: Outline meal times, snack availability, and any dietary restrictions.
- Screen time: Do you want to set limits on device usage and designate screen-free zones such as bedrooms, or at the dining table.

Communication and Boundaries:

- House rules: Clearly outline expectations for behaviour, noise levels, guest policies, etc.

- Communication preferences: Explain how you prefer to be communicated with and understand how they prefer to be communicated with.
- Respecting privacy: Discuss knocking on doors, personal space, and boundaries with belongings.
- Feelings and emotional needs: Reassure the child they can talk about their feelings openly and honestly.
- Conflict resolution: Develop a process for handling disagreements calmly and respectfully.
- Triggers and coping mechanisms: Discuss whether the child has any specific triggers or needs support managing emotions.

Additional Considerations:

- Medical needs: Include information on medications, allergies, and doctors' appointments.
- School and activities: List contact information for schools, extracurricular activities and teachers.
- Culture and religion: Show respect for the child's cultural background and religious practices.

Bonus:

- Fun section: Add a section where the child can add their favourite activities, restaurants, or things to do in the area.

- Glossary of terms: If there are terms specific to your household define them for clarity.

Remember to give the child plenty of time to learn these new habits and try not to overwhelm them with too much information at once. Be patient with the child. Imagine you are a young person trying to learn a hundred new habits at once. Sometimes your placement may not even be long enough to learn a single one. Some children who are moved around the system frequently give up trying to understand the unwritten rules, and if they meet with negative responses when they get things wrong, they disengage with attempting to get it right.

1.3 The Guardrails Within Which I Find Freedom

Along with unwritten rules come boundaries. For many children in care boundaries have often been either non-existent or severe. They often have not learnt to navigate the subtleties of when they should and shouldn't challenge these things. Challenging boundaries can be a healthy behaviour. When I went into care I was in a state of extreme compliance. My ten years prior had taught me to obey without question. Often just the fear of disobedience and the potential consequences were enough to keep me doing as I was told. Trying my best to keep everyone happy. When I left care, I failed to understand how to build boundaries and where I needed to push back and challenge the expectations placed on me. There is a level of healthy challenge children can explore in their worlds. This exploration teaches them the importance of not only respect for others but respect for themselves.

Communicating the rules and expectations of the family is important. As is giving space to challenge, question and occasionally push back. If you find a child constantly challenging boundaries, remember for them control may have once been a survival need. Being forced into a totally different world where compliance is not harmful can take a long time to assimilate. When considering boundaries keep in mind the following important factors.

Communication and Collaboration:

- **Open communication:** Creating a safe space for open and honest communication is key. Let the child know they can talk to you about anything, including their feelings about the rules. Remember a huge amount of our communication is not with words. If they appear uncomfortable gently enquire why and help them to express their feelings.
- **Joint effort:** Whenever possible, involve the child in creating the house rules. This fosters a sense of ownership and increases the likelihood they'll follow the rules. Where you already have an established set of rules try to find those where you can compromise and build a shared agreement.
- **Focus on understanding:** Before setting rules, try to understand the child's background and experiences.

This can help you tailor expectations and address any underlying anxieties. It may help with understanding their reaction to any rule setting.

Clarity and Consistency:

- **Clear expectations:** Make sure the rules are clear, concise, and easy to understand. Use age-appropriate language and visuals if needed. When discussing rules you can ask them to repeat-back to you what you discussed. This is a great way of checking understanding. None of us like to appear stupid and will sometimes claim we understand even when we don't.
- **Consistency is key:** Enforce the rules consistently. Wavering between strictness and laxity creates confusion and undermines the rules. It can quickly create a space where the uncertainty of what we should be doing drives a natural disregard.
- **Positive reinforcement:** Focus on catching the child following the rules and offer praise or rewards. This reinforces positive behaviour. It is much more effective to focus on and build the right behaviours. Though be careful not to over-praise or it can lose its value.

Establishing Trust and Security:

- **Focus on building trust:** A strong bond with the foster parent is essential for a child to accept boundaries. It may not be appropriate to launch straight into rules or to cover all expectations at once. Start small and explore what their expectations are.

- **Be patient:** It takes time for a child in foster care to adjust to a new environment and new rules. Be patient and understanding. Just imagine you woke up one day and were thrown into a totally new job with no under-standing of the people or the processes. You would get it wrong too.
- **Focus on safety:** The primary purpose of rules is to ensure the child's safety and wellbeing. Explain the rea-soning behind the rules whenever possible. Offering a reason why or asking them why they think some rules may exist is a good way to build understanding.

Over the years I have continued learning how healthy boundaries serve me and those around me. From studying great examples and the wealth of literature in the world I have established my own boundaries in how I spend my time, and what I allow others to bring into my space. These boundaries are difficult to hold at times as I feel the echo of guilt. I fear I may be failing someone or letting them down. I hope that what I am actually doing is giving them permission and opportunity to create their own boundaries. To learn to inhabit their world in a way which feels right for them.

1.4 Summary

Rules and boundaries can be complex and change over time. As some final thoughts to help you find the right balance consider:

- **Starting slowly:** Don't overwhelm the child with too many rules at once. Focus on the most important ones initially.
- **Acknowledging feelings**: Validate the child's feelings about the rules. It's okay for them to feel frustrated or confused at times.
- **Flexibility:** There will be times when flexibility is needed. Be prepared to adjust the rules based on the child's progress and changing needs. Changing and adapting rules is not the same as being lax.
- **Seek support:** Don't be afraid to seek support from your social worker, a therapist or another trusted person if you're having difficulty establishing boundaries with your foster child.
- **Challenge back:** One foster child proudly told me how their foster mother challenged the rule she was not allowed to give them fizzy drinks. If you are advised to follow rules for the child which feel unnecessary or unhelpful, challenge back.

Rules and boundaries can sometimes feel unachievable for the child. When their experience has been significantly different to those expectations in a home, they can find themselves often making mistakes. If you find yourself frustrated with the amount of challenge, consider whether they are trying and failing. They may not always admit they have tried, having learnt it is better to present a strong and determined front than admit when they got something wrong.

I was often happy to admit when I got something wrong. What others couldn't see was that no one would chastise me more than myself. I would find a space alone and tell myself how stupid I was, over and over, afraid of what might happen if I kept failing to get it right. Fearful I would be moved to another home. When you try and fail it reinforces the belief you are not good enough. Not good enough to be in that setting, with that family, in the life someone is trying to offer you. Reassure any foster child we all make mistakes and get things wrong. It is the fact that we find a way to keep trying which matters most. I am sure I have made hundreds of mistakes over my lifetime. I did all the things you may expect of a teen in my position. It was the chances I was given to learn from my mistakes which contributed to no blunder becoming a predictor of my future. I would not be where I am today without making some of those missteps, or without the kindness of others to support me in trying again.

CHAPTER 2

I Might Say I Am Okay, But I Am Not

It is hard to describe the feeling of fear when you are faced with the unknown. I don't think we as human beings are built to adjust very well to a totally new environment overnight. To be taken away from everything you know. By the time I went in to care I had already known what it was like to be a breath away from death. I lived in a world of uncertainty, not knowing if I would come home to find my mum covered in blood, surrounded by doctors. I was never sure if what I said or did would create a chain reaction which forced her decline or triggered my father. Yet somehow in all that tumultuous chaos there was some level of familiarity. A level of certainty which gave the illusion of control whilst my life was spiralling away.

I remember the first day we went to our foster home. In the car on the way there the social worker turned to me and quietly said, "Be careful of the other foster child. She cracked open another child's head last week with a metal talc can. Best you give her some space." I just nodded silently and added the information to my very limited store of knowledge about where I was going. I am sure at times it was apparent I was not okay, but I also know there were plenty of occasions when to the rest of the world I appeared fine. Inside I was so afraid that I could feel an icy fire pulsing through my body. I lived in an almost constant state of fear. I was afraid of the past, the present and the future. Afraid of getting it all wrong and afraid of getting it right.

Many children in care experience deep and complex challenges with their emotions and mental health. I wish my foster parents had been more aware of what I was struggling with. In those moments after a visit to mum or when I didn't want to return to my father, I wish someone had noticed my inner turmoil. That they might have sat with me whilst I struggled. Being alone with your thoughts, be they good or bad, is one of the most isolating feelings in the world. Here are some suggestions of things we can do to help notice and support a child in our care.

2.1 Keeping an Eye Out

- **Little signs:** Just noticing if the child is a little quieter, or perhaps more animated than normal. Those subtle changes in demeanour may be slight but they are often an indicator of a greater struggle inside. Most of the time I tried to hide what I was feeling. I was trying to detach myself. If my feelings were apparent, I was already well past the point at which I could have benefited from some support.

- **Changes in behaviour:** At one point I started sleep-walking. I remember scaring the life out of my foster sister one night. We were sharing a room and she was extremely concerned when I climbed the wardrobe to manically tidy the teddies on the top. Whilst it may be normal for a child to go through many changes in behaviour, be aware of the fact that a change in behaviour for a foster child may be an indicator of something they need help addressing.

2.2 Connection before Correction

Trust me: I get it, the way I described things as a child was not always right. I didn't have the words at times, and when I did my lack of ability to articulate a situation meant I sounded uncertain, confused or unbelievable. Please understand the lack of a child's ability to explain many things is simply because they don't have the words or that they are very upset. Even if a child has remembered something incorrectly, or heaven forbid a child is outright lying, the reality is there is a reason they are trying to communicate this to you. The damage done by any lack of belief is far greater than the risk of misplacing your trust.

Don't trust me: Yes, I have intentionally written these two statements in absolute conflict with each other. There were many times people would ask me if I was okay and I would simply nod along. There were a hundred reasons why I didn't always answer truthfully. Sometimes I did not understand what I was feeling. If I didn't understand it how could I explain it? Sometimes I thought being honest about how I felt would result in something I didn't want. If I told you how afraid I was of going to see my mum would you stop me seeing her? Sometimes I just wanted to retreat, and I knew the quickest way to do that was to find the path of least resistance. If you sense a child is not being honest about how they feel, ask again in a different way. If-they still resist it is probably best in the moment to give them some space. If you keep feeling that they are refusing or failing to communicate how they feel, help them learn a better way to approach those moments.

2.3 Unhelpful Coping Mechanisms

When I was in care I used many approaches to help manage or often dissociate with my emotions. Some of the methods were less positive than others. I am sharing some of them so we can be aware of those things which may happen and the need to encourage healthy coping mechanisms.

Self-Harm: In all the time I self-harmed no one ever knew. There was some enquiry at one point after my father found a piece of school homework, but the reality is I hid my self-harm very well. For some this action can be more obvious. It is absolutely something to take seriously and embed additional support with as quickly as possible. I managed to hold back from the worst extents of self-harm but for many it can quickly spiral or become an inescapable need.

Smoking: Everyone in the house knew my foster sister smoked and she would get in all sorts of trouble about it. For the longest time no one realised I smoked too. The first time I had a cigarette was before I went into care. One night after there had been huge arguments and lots of violence in the house, I found myself in tears on the doorstep of a friend. She was a wonderful friend though much older than me. That night she walked with me in the dark and tried to ask what had happened. I failed to explain what had transpired, so she sat on the concrete steps at the end of our street in silence with me as I lost myself in the pain. That was the first night I ever smoked. I think she was desperate to help and had no idea how, so offered me one of her cigarettes. Smoking absolutely developed into a coping mechanism.

There can be many other unhelpful coping mechanisms, including drugs, truancy, crime. They can all offer a sense of release, control or belonging which short term feel like the only way to continue. It is important to try to establish what the child is getting from these actions to support them in finding a better alternative.

2.4 Helpful Coping Mechanisms

Ask them what would help: Sometimes a child might have an idea of what would help. Perhaps the opportunity to write things down, to have a safe space, to go for a walk. When they are struggling let the child explore what works for them.

Role model the right behaviour: It's okay if you find it hard at times too. Helping a child learn and understand that everyone struggles is so important. When I look back, I want to see the examples of people working through challenges in a healthy way. If you engage in practices to help you through those difficult moments share them with the child so they can learn from you. If you need to retreat or create some space for yourself, make sure to explain to the child it is not about them. It is your need to manage your own emotions. Reassure them that you will be back once you have been able to calm down. It is very easy for a child to blame themselves and feel guilty for causing upset.

Connect them with a therapist: Therapy can provide a safe space to explore past trauma and develop a more positive self-image. I have engaged in therapy a few times in my life. Sometimes it has been simply life changing, but sometimes it has been awful. If a child has previously engaged in therapy and had a bad experience, encourage them to try again. Not all therapies or indeed therapists are the same.

Singing: This was a huge one for me. I was a member of the choir. I would sing anywhere and everywhere. To this day I find if I am really struggling singing can somehow override it all. I can't hold a thought and a song in my head at the same time. Sometimes my foster sister and I would go to the park and sit on the bench just singing Disney songs for hours. Even when I started work the team would often tease me for singing at my desk.

Creative outlet: It might not be everyone's cup of tea, but poetry was always there for me. I loved the freedom of the words not having to make entire sense. Being raised on a diet of

Disney meant rhyme came very naturally. For others it may be journalling, or painting, or cross stitch. My foster mum taught me to cross stitch, and I loved the meditative state of counting stitches on a sheet. With all of these things there is something about creating something from nothing and shaping our feelings into something more tangible. Making real the things we fail to explain. Arts and music have been found to have a huge benefit on those who have been through traumatic events.

Sport: The benefits of taking up a sport go far beyond the impact of exercise on our physical and mental health. Team sports help us to build relationships and learn to work together. Even more individual based sports like archery can invite us into a community of people with a shared interest around which we can build connection.

2.5 Potentially Helpful Coping Mechanisms

School/Work: I absolutely threw myself in to school back then. Partly because it was the space I felt safest in. Partly because I found an addiction to learning. There was so much of my world I didn't understand. So much I couldn't work out. I found a desire to understand everything I could in the hope that one day I might stumble across an answer. Even now when I struggle, I find such solace in work. In doing a job I know and love. In the complex simplicity of thinking through a solution to a problem. But therein lies the potential downside. In focusing on the bits I feel I can solve, I am avoiding the things which feel too hard to tackle. You can only avoid a problem for so long before it becomes too big to escape. Finding a focus in which a child can achieve success, be it academics, sports or something entirely different, can be hugely valuable. Just ensure it is not at the cost of working through the real problems.

Faith: This had been a tenet of my life for the entire time before foster care. From an extremely Catholic family which was well embedded in the church and a Catholic education, faith had been a constant in the chaos. I was really lucky in many ways to have that grounding. On nights I was afraid I would pull out the tiny New Testament which I kept by my bed, and I would follow the index to read stories about how Jesus calmed the storm or welcomed everyone into his arms. This mythical person who in the best ways offered hope and kindness. I would sometimes sneak into church on my own and just sit breathing in the hints of wood, stone and smoke. When I went into care I lost a lot of that faith. No one ever asked me if I ever wanted to go to church, or if I would like to say a prayer.

Faith is such a unique thing. We often consider it in relation to religion. It can also be about faith in a person or in a less tangible higher power. Even within a religion the ways someone chooses to practice their faith can vary hugely. If you can understand whether the child you are caring for holds any beliefs or rituals and find a way to help them hold on to that (if they want to) it can be a huge benefit. It does not mean you have to convert or carry out the actions with them. Perhaps you can find another member of their faith to support them. Even just giving them time and space and recognising their beliefs can be of huge benefit.

The flip side for me was that my faith hugely reinforced my belief everything was all my fault. There is a prayer at the start of every Mass, 'Through my fault, my fault, my most grievous fault. In what I have done and what I have failed to do...' My faith gave me huge comfort and caused me great pain. I would still however choose to have held on to that belief for the time I did because I know in the moments I felt most alone, I always felt like someone else was there.

2.6 Summary

Coping mechanisms are something we all have to differing levels in response to the challenges in our lives. There is value in adapting the approach to the individual child and working out what will be sustainable for you too. Be patient and understanding, not just with the child but also with yourself as you navigate a new relationship and potentially difficult circumstances. The emotional journey of a foster child can be a tricky thing to navigate for both the carer and the child. Emotions such as anxiety, fear, hurt, sadness are often expected effects of the things they have experienced. Sometimes common reactions like anger and disobedience are not associated with the trauma but with the child. When I was in care, I remember lots of conversations I would overhear or be invited into. Commonly when they were discussing me being sad or anxious they would say things like "Row is struggling because the visit with her mum was cancelled." Or "Row appears anxious about visiting her father." These sets of emotions would be associated with an event. But when it came to things like anger, we were just labelled with no association with what may be causing it. I believe all behaviour is rooted in emotion and sometimes it is not clear what emotion is driving a child. Our emotions can lead to an array of behaviour. Often children are more emotionally driven, so if you are seeing a behaviour which is challenging it is always worth exploring what emotion sits behind it. Any effort to help them build a healthy relationship with their emotions will pay dividends in the long run and can make a huge impact to their lives.

CHAPTER 3

I Am Not Worthy

I once spoke with a parent who was confused about their foster child pushing to return to her biological family. The child had experienced terrible abuse in that home and was not guaranteed a safe, stable environment to return to. She had been settled and with the foster parents for years. They could not fathom why she wished to return to her biological parents. They asked what I thought they might have done wrong. They couldn't wrap their heads around the fact they most likely had done everything right. That there is just something about feeling like you don't belong which lingers in you as a child taken away from your family.

I often had that feeling when I was in care. It went beyond feeling like a guest in someone else's home. It was a deep innate sense that I didn't belong. Worse still that I was not worthy of the family I found myself in. When the time came that I felt I had no choice but to return home a part of me was heartbroken. I cried myself to sleep that first night. I knew I would never have that sense of safety again. I grieved not only for the happiness I had lost but for the future I would never have. But there was also a part of me that felt it was inevitable, in fact even natural. I had returned to the place I belonged. Along with all the fear and abuse it felt right somehow. I didn't want it to feel that way, but it did.

For all the kindness I was shown in my time in care, I never really learnt to find a sense of self-worth. Knowing I was a waste of space made it easy to slip back into the world which re-inforced that belief. I didn't feel that sense of friction anymore. The world once more told me I was worthless, and I knew it was true. Now I look back and think that was crazy. I was such a good kid, kind, hardworking, loving. Yet there at my core was a void which consumed all possibility of positive self-worth. It is so important to nurture a sense of self-worth in the children we care for. That relationship they hold with themselves is the foundation from which many things grow. Here are some examples of behaviours you may notice in a child with a lack of self-worth.

3.1 Recognising a Lack of Self Worth.
Verbal Cues:

- **Negative self-talk:** They may constantly put themselves down, sometimes using obvious phrases like "I'm stupid," "I'm worthless," or "I'll never amount to anything." The negative self-talk I articulated was much more subtle. I would often comment "It's not good enough", whether I was referring to homework or the tidiness of my room. I think if you substituted 'it's' with an 'I' you would have heard what I was feeling. Instead of "It's not good enough" I was saying "I'm not good enough".

- **Blaming themselves:** They might take responsibility for negative events, even if they were not at fault. This was one I hugely carried. My father actually told me outright I was the reason he had to divorce my mother. But I carried every single painful reality from my past as my sole responsibility. For every situation I could find something I did or failed to do which caused it. After a long time of people just telling me, "Don't be silly, it's not your fault." "Of course it was nothing to do with you." I stopped saying it aloud, but I never stopped thinking it.

- **Difficulty accepting compliments:** When complimented they may brush it off, deny it, or deflect with a negative comment about themselves. I have had varying success with compliments over the years. I think my inability to accept a compliment came much later after I had left care. But there was always a lack of them landing; like a stone skimming water, they never really found a home.

- **Extreme reactions to others:** A child who maybe highlights every good thing someone else does and offers immense praise could be struggling with self-belief. Equally criticising every action of someone or bullying others can be an outward response to a lack of inner belief.

Behavioural Cues:

- **Isolation and withdrawal:** They may avoid social interaction and prefer to be alone, fearing rejection. I think when we think of this behaviour we think of the extreme and pronounced slamming of doors or refusing to come out of a room. But it can be as simple as politely declining to engage in family activities.
- **People-pleasing:** They might go to great lengths to please others, even at their own expense, seeking validation. I hate to admit that I absolutely did this at times. I like to think that my behaviour was not always as a result of wanting to please others, but at times it certainly was. Whether I was agreeing to go and stay with my father or trying for that better grade in school, many of the times I was doing something outside of my comfort zone it was for others and not for me.
- **Risk-taking behaviours:** They could engage in risky or dangerous activities, acting out of a sense of worthlessness or self-punishment. This is a hard one to explain but if you feel that you are only worthy of punishment then creating the circumstances in which that punishment is inevitable feels like an inescapable fate. The minor control you had in drawing that conclusion nearer was the only ounce of certainty you could find. I would often hear foster children say, "I may as well…" like the conclusion was only going to arrive anyway so why not

accelerate its completion, get it over with or at least try to find some fun or comfort along the way.

- **Changes in appetite**: These can be signs of underlying emotional distress that could be linked to self-worth issues. When I returned to my father's and the abuse started getting worse, I found myself eating very little. I lost a lot of weight and whilst others complimented my new figure, I was lost in a world of finding food a sickening idea. For most of my life the greater struggle has been binge eating till I felt sick. I didn't associate the discomfort I caused myself as anything associated with my self-worth, but it was there.

- **Academic decline:** They may lose motivation in school, neglecting their studies as a way of confirming their negative self-beliefs. This can lead to a dangerous downwards cycle: "I am not worthy, so I will not try, I do not try so I only fail, I fail and so I am not worthy." I had always been an academic over achiever. Sadly, I dropped out before completing my A Levels, partly because I was being bullied in school, but also because I had concluded there was no chance I would ever get to go to university. When I was offered full time employment it was an obvious choice. Now if I was faced with that decision again, I would fight for university. I have always loved to learn and whilst I eventually got to complete my Masters degree, giving up on that dream so early was one of my biggest regrets.

- **New inappropriate relationships:** Perhaps they have started hanging around with new people who feel like unusual or risky company. They may be withholding information about their relationships. Spending more time in chat rooms or online. Choosing to engage in a persona which fills a need and bolsters their self-worth. I am ashamed to admit this was a path I tracked for a while as a teenager. I met a guy online who seemed genuinely interested in me. I spent hours speaking to him every week and even accepted money from him when he offered to treat me to a gift. After months of sending pictures (not all of which were appropriate) and talking online I agreed to meet. Gratefully I was not foolish enough to meet him alone. When I refused to have sex with him I never heard from him again.

Other Signs:

- **Physical appearance:** Neglecting hygiene or appearance could indicate a lack of self-care and low self-esteem. Sometimes children in care have not been taught the basics of hygiene or grooming. If they are offered the guidance and still struggle to manage to care for themselves in this way, it could be a sign of a lack of self-worth. I remember one foster child often saying, "Who cares?" if anyone complained about their appearance. I suspect the reality was they didn't care enough about themselves to find the energy to try.

- **Possessiveness:** They might cling to possessions or become overly attached to them, seeking a sense of security. It can appear unreasonable that they place so much importance in items. With a lack of self-worth comes a vulnerability that if you lose the things you own, not only will you be nothing, you will have nothing.
- **Difficulty making decisions**: They may struggle to make choices, fearing making the wrong decision and reinforcing their sense of inadequacy. They may feel the impact of every decision is a direct reflection of their self-worth. Either reinforcing the lack of it or creating a chasm between the positive impact and who they are, which in turns builds a fear of being able to achieve that outcome again.

It's important to remember that these signs can also be indicative of other issues. If you notice a combination of these behaviours, or you are ever worried about a child's behaviour, it's a good idea to talk to the child and explore what might be going on. You can always reach out for additional support if you think the child would benefit from extra help.

3.2 Building Self-Worth

I don't think any amount of someone telling me how great I was would have changed my perspective. For all the relationships I built the one I really needed to nurture was the one with myself. I wish I had found the ability to love myself, even just a little. That the future I couldn't bear to dream of was possible. Someone said to me recently the most powerful thing we can do is carry someone's hope when it is too hard for them to bear. Without self-worth when so much of your future depends on you alone, hope is sacrificed. Without hope there is no possibility and without possibility there is no reason to try. Helping a child find that self-belief can enable them to build a foundation from which behaviour, achievements and happiness can grow. There are plenty of ways you can try and help a child build their self-worth.

Focus on Strengths and Achievements

- **Identify strengths**: Help the child identify their unique talents and skills. This could be anything from artistic ability to athleticism, problem-solving skills, or a kind heart. Sometimes there will be an obvious ability you can nurture. For other children this may be a journey of discovery. If a child really feels they have no strengths find ways to expose them to new and varied environments, situations and people. Help them discover what strengths lie at their core.

- **Celebrate achievements:** Acknowledge and celebrate their accomplishments, big or small. This could be a good grade on a test, winning a game, mastering a new skill, or simply completing a chore. Be careful to balance recognising actual achievements and not just praising everything they do. If you overpraise it can actually reinforce the negative belief as they question why you think that easy thing is something worth special recognition.

- **Offer opportunities for success**: Provide the child with opportunities to experience success in areas they are interested in. This could involve enrolling them in extracurricular activities, assigning them age-appropriate chores, or giving them leadership roles. This can expose them to more failure but that is an important element of building self-worth. Some level of risk of failure allows us to feel the achievement. Try to set the opportunities/chore/activity at a level which is not super easy or extremely difficult.

- **Encouragement:** Offer encouragement when the child faces challenges. Let them know you believe in their ability to succeed, even if they don't always get it right the first time. Keep them focused on the end goal. Remind them of similar occasions they have struggled and still got there. Ask them how it felt when they achieved the goal.

- **Focus on effort:** Praise the child's effort and perseverance, not just the final outcome. This teaches them that hard work is valuable, regardless of the result. Break down the goal into smaller objectives. It could be as something as small as "Tonight we can just watch the boys play football and then next week you can join in." Find a level of challenge which does not push them too far too fast.

- **Let them see you fail:** Let them understand we all fail at times. Talk about examples when you have got it wrong. Or when you fail show them how you will try again.

- **Give them a win:** If they are really struggling you may want to create an opportunity where you expect them to succeed. Or try something new together where everyone has equal opportunity to fail.
- **Help them be okay with failing:** A brilliant social worker told me once he always plays Frustration with a child who is struggling with losing. He found that the game removed all elements of skill and provided a great way to work through the uncertainty and reality of luck alone.

Building Self-Esteem Activities:

- **Creative outlets:** Encourage the child to explore creative outlets like art, music, writing, or drama. These activities can help them express themselves and develop a sense of accomplishment.
- **Community service:** Volunteer together or help others in your community. This can give the child a sense of purpose and belonging. Find out what they would like to help with. Perhaps they care for animals and could volunteer to walk dogs at the shelter, or maybe they enjoy music and could run an hour at the hospital radio station.

- **Role models:** Provide the child with positive role models who they can look up to. These could be real people they know or fictional characters in books or movies. Talking about what makes these role models great and the challenges they may have faced to get where they are can help.
- **Sport/ physical activity:** Sport can provide a great way to develop skill and offer autonomy over your body. Any activity however unusual can provide benefits in building self-esteem.
- **Family affirmations:** Build collective affirmations which can acknowledge failure and inspire achievement. Our family moto is 'If at first you don't succeed, try, try again.' Both my girls roll their eyes now when I mention it. I know that in the past that saying has helped them pick themselves up on many an occasion.
- **Recognise the small things:** Self-esteem is built and maintained in the small everyday actions and achievements. Recognise and acknowledge a child for the things they do, little acts of kindness or achievements in their day. A consistent regular recognition of their capabilities will build a solid foundation over time.

Additional Tips:

- **Be patient:** Building self-worth takes time and consistency. Don't get discouraged if you don't see results immediately.

- **Be a positive role model:** Children learn by example. Show the child what it means to have self-worth by practising self-compassion and positive self-talk yourself.
- **Seek professional help:** If you're concerned about the child's self-worth, consider seeking professional help from a therapist or counsellor. I only truly learned to shape my sense of self-worth through the support of a brilliant therapist.

3.3 Summary

There were many occasions when I would feel that sense of worthlessness. For instance, the time I had to make my own dress for the school disco and by the end of the night the seams had started falling apart. That shabby sense of shame ever apparent. Or the occasions it would be a friend's birthday and I had little to offer them in the way of gifts. The black bag of toys to no one turning up to watch the school show, or teachers stating I couldn't be in care because I was too good. The risk is once you find yourself in that head space you unknowingly seek out examples which reinforce that belief. Helping a child to recognise their strengths and self-worth can teach them not to look to the world for validation. Many of the children in care turn to unwanted avenues to achieve that sense of worth. I have spoken with children who have experienced gangs or returned to abusive environments. Beyond that sense of connection and belonging there is also often an element of "I am playing my part, I have a purpose or a value."

I still to this day find I am sensitive to that need to feel I am adding value and doing a good job. In many ways that desire has helped my career as I seek out new opportunities when I find I am not helping the team or business as much as I feel I need too. I am sure perhaps it sits behind a lot of my drive for charitable work as I desperately seek to have a positive impact on the world. When I do find myself lost in those moments of a lack of self belief I turn to others I admire and respect. Hearing their recognition of where I have made a difference before helps quieten that voice that I am not good enough.

CHAPTER 4

Treat Me Just the Same

There was one computer in my foster parents' house. Their son was kind enough to let me use it. I found a new joy building pyramids and managing imaginary cities as I whiled away hours losing myself in the needs of an Egyptian kingdom. Until one day my foster mother decided I could not use the computer anymore. I am sure there were many reasons behind her decision. Ultimately for me it meant I had no access to a computer in my foster home and that was the end of my adventures. There were many examples of being treated like a foster child rather than just a child.

The other occasion which always stuck with me was when I came to the point of deciding on A Levels in high school. I had the potential to be a straight A student. I achieved all grade B's and A's in my GCSE's. I wanted to study four A levels, Biology, Chemistry, Physics and Geography. At first my teachers refused. Even though I had the required grades to study four subjects they insisted I should only do three. Their reason, "You have too much on your plate already, as a foster child you should manage your expectations." It took three meetings with my teachers, head of year and deputy head to convince them I should be allowed. They cared about the potential impact on my mental health. They wanted me to go easier on myself. Although no one ever said "You don't belong here", every example of a difference in treatment was another piece of evidence that I didn't fit. I didn't have the thing I longed for most, a family to truly call my own and a life more ordinary.

Some children in care I have spoken with talked about their preference of residential care because at least there they weren't given the false hope of being part of a family or treated like a second-rate citizen. There are of course times when we cannot avoid treating children differently. Even now my eldest will complain that her younger sister has easier chores, and the youngest is unhappy that she has to go to bed much earlier. Setting aside obvious differences like age there are many other reasons you may need to treat a child differently. Where it is essential it is important to be clear on the reasons why. There are lots of spaces where a disparity of treatment can impact a foster child. Some of the spaces where there is particular value in reflecting on a consistent approach may include the following.

4.1 Daily Life

Disciplinary Measures: Disciplinary approaches may differ. This is a tricky space as foster parents might be more hesitant to use harsh punishments for fear of jeopardising a placement. I have encountered examples where foster carers have been advised they cannot use the same disciplinary measures for foster children as they would for their own. One foster carer I know was told they could not confiscate a mobile phone, even though this was an approach they used at times with their own child. The challenge here can be that inconsistent punishment can result in the foster child not actually feeling as much love as the biological child. They can perceive a lack of consistent treatment as "You don't really care about me and my behaviour."

A lack of appropriate consequences for children can also create additional hurdles as they transition into the world of independence. The world is unlikely to provide easier treatment due to their circumstances. In my experience unless there is a specific issue or reason not to be consistent then this should be the goal.

Household Rules: All rules for children will require periods of flexibility. Sometimes rules for any child may need to be relaxed or indeed more strictly applied. You wouldn't expect a child to carry out their chores when they are ill or behave to the same standard if they had an upsetting visit with a family member. The goal here is a consistent approach. If you relax the rules for one child for a reason you should do the same for any other.

Physical Affection: This is a minefield. When I was in care foster carers were trained to give sideways hugs. To limit all physical contact to eradicate the possibility that any contact was inappropriate. Even recently I have spoken with a foster carer who was advised that she should not sit on the bed to read a young child a bedtime story but that she should pull up a chair beside the bed. For me as a blanket approach this risks being really damaging advice. There have been numerous studies which have demonstrated over and over the importance of physical contact, nurturing physical affection and touch. It is always worth being mindful that a biological child might receive more casual physical affection like hugs or kisses, and this will be noticed. We talk a little more about touch in the later chapter 'I need to feel loved'.

Family Traditions: It is really valuable to go the extra mile to include a foster child in any household traditions. Before the event take the time to talk to the child about what to expect and the role they can play. That extra preparation can be the difference between an opportunity to build on a relationship or the child feeling more excluded due to a lack of understanding of what to do. Don't assume that common traditions like the Easter bunny or Christmas traditions like crackers are something the child has experienced before. It is equally important to create opportunities to engage in any traditions the child has and would like to keep practising.

Unconscious Bias: Foster parents might unconsciously show favouritism towards their biological children, allocating more time or attention to them. This may be a very natural thing to do. Just being mindful of the risk and trying to balance it with time with the foster child can help ensure they don't feel less worthy of your time.

4.2 Special Events and Activities

Family Vacations: It was very common in the foster family I was in that we would not always go on the main family holidays. If there are financial constraints, please reach out to social services or charities to try to secure funding. If the need is to "have a break from the child" please be mindful of the impact this narrative can have. Approach any conversation with the child very carefully. Do not use language like "we need a break", or "we need to get away". These often seemingly harmless statements can create a deep-seated sense of rejection and fear. Where possible always take foster children on holiday with you, if absolutely not possible discuss with the child clear plans for their care whilst you are away and plan how to reengage with the child on your return. Talk about what they might like to do when you get back. Perhaps you can engage in a favourite pastime with them when you return. Ensure they understand the priority is making sure they are well cared for while you are away.

Extracurricular Activities: When I speak with foster parents about clubs and hobbies for children the barriers are often not financial but due to demands already placed on the carers' time. For many foster children there will be additional appointments to navigate. Challenges with maintaining family connections or extra time meeting with social workers. Some foster parents I have spoken with have told me they are focused on supporting school performance, mental health and just getting the child on track. I cannot stress enough the importance and benefit for everyone from engaging a child in extracurricular activities.

When I was fostered I was a member of the Air Training Corp (A.T.C.). The opportunities that group gave me in nurturing my skills and building my confidence stayed with me. It was the only space I had where I was treated just like any other child. I found myself through being a cadet. I did things I never thought I could do, I made friends and I learnt more about myself in those few hours every week than I did at any other time in my life. Nurturing a passion or interest for a child, whether they enjoy sports, music, or something entirely different can create a sense of self and help build numerous healthy relationships for the child.

Family Gatherings: Larger family gatherings can be difficult for a foster child to navigate. They may not have experienced a similar setting before. The expectations of how to behave aren't always clear. There can also be lots of people they don't know, which can increase anxiety. It can help to share some photos of the people attending beforehand. Make sure to mention the quirky behaviours they might expect to see. Give them a sense of what large gatherings are usually like. Are they loud and very fluid or does everyone take turns to update the group in a very measured way?

Explore how the child might feel at the gathering, and if it feels helpful talk through ways they might be able to navigate any difficult feelings if they come up. Perhaps they could retreat to their room for a little while and agree when you will check in on them, or maybe if it is in a restaurant you could offer to take a short walk together. Family gatherings can often be a melting pot for stories old and new. These settings can be really hard for some children if something gets mentioned which triggers an upsetting memory or they become overwhelmed. It can also help to consider preparing family members by informing them of the best ways to support any child.

Gifts and Special Occasions: There is a whole chapter of this book dedicated to the fact that it is not about presents, but what can cause damage is a significant and persistent variation in the amount or type of gifts. When I was in care I still had contact with my biological parents. Contact with my mother was only in person a handful of times a year and always heavily supervised. Contact with my father was more regular, we would stay with him every other weekend. We always received presents from both of our biological parents as well as our foster parents, so effectively had three Christmases or birthdays. I didn't ever notice if I received less in comparison to their biological children or other foster children. The number of gifts I received was never really something I noted. I do remember the time they bought me a pair of roller blades because I wanted to skate like my older foster sister. I never managed to be half as good as her, but I remember feeling proud trying. I am sure it was not the most expensive gift I received in my life, but it stuck with me. I loved the thoughtfulness of the gift. For many children a disparity in gift giving, especially if it is obvious and persistent, can reinforce their lack of self-worth. If there are financial constraints try to be balanced or discreet in your gift giving. Always explain if there is a reason they can't have the one thing they want.

4.3 Communicating Why

Sometimes a difference in treatment is unavoidable. Rather than allowing this to be perceived as unfairness or a lack of care, it is important to communicate why. The perception of fairness is influenced by many things. Some things we can control such as the decisions we make. Other elements are out of our control such as the experiences the child already has. Where possible, to enable a positive outcome, it is worth ensuring you are building healthy and effective communication with the child. Sometimes feeling you are being treated unfairly is just a lack of communication. An inability of the child to articulate how they feel or for the carer to provide the reason. Here are some lessons I have learnt in my time communicating with children.

- **Don't assume:** Don't assume you might know what is going on for the child and what has caused it. Don't say things like "I know whenever you visit your mum you feel like you let her down." Or "Don't be upset that you can't go home for Christmas." It is possible even if a child has clearly articulated their feelings about a similar event before, those feelings may have changed.
- **Open-ended questions:** Ask open ended questions, "Can you tell me more about what's going on for you?" or "Is there anything that's bothering you?" Even if we

think we know the cause of an upset, helping the child to articulate that for themselves and name what they are feeling can help to establish emotional intelligence and a sense of trust.

- **Active listening:** Active listening includes summarising and repeating back to the child what you think you heard and asking questions to gently probe further. Avoid telling the child what they should be feeling. Recognise and reaffirm their experience.

- **Give validation:** Even if the action is not something you can condone, you can express that you understand their feelings and that it is okay for them to feel that way. Validating feelings does not mean they will be stuck with the feeling or that you will make it worse.

4.4 Summary

There is a common misunderstanding between equality (treating everyone the same) and equity (treating everyone in a way which allows them the same opportunity). It is important to remember that for all the desire to treat foster children the same, they will each hold a very unique set of experiences and challenges. They may feel they have little say or control over their lives. Whilst all children will have a limited control often based on their age or maturity, there are more occasions in a foster child's life when significantly impactful choices are taken out of their hands. This can result in fear of the future, a sense of diminished power, frustration and anger.

Many foster children will also face a greater uncertainty about the future. When I was fostered, I could only manage two extremes when considering the future. Sometimes I could imagine this happily ever after where all the trauma and troubles melted away. Often, I could only imagine nothing. There was no middle ground. No grasp of potential outcomes. And occasionally there was only fear. So much fear that it was a fight to get through the minutes let alone the days.

All of these realities and more can mean it is appropriate and necessary to treat a foster child differently. Just try to ensure when they are treated differently it is driven by a desire to support them and do what is best for them. Of course, they may not always agree with this, and in the moment they may resent or act out against their care. In the longer term, if you can hold true to being led by care they will look back and know those around them had their best interests at heart.

CHAPTER 5

Help Me Shape a Passion

When so much of the focus is on keeping a child safe, ensuring their education and trying to settle them in a home, a school, a life, sometimes the child is lost in it all. They likely will not have had a strong sense of self before coming into care. If they do, this sense of self may be entangled in all sorts of beliefs which do not serve them and will hold them back from being happy and successful.

When a child goes into care there is often a clear focus to help establish positive routines, boundaries, environments and relationships. I would suggest it is equally important to help the child build a relationship with themselves. Whilst stripping away the negative aspects of their lives it is important to fill the void which is left behind. I struggled in the beginning when everyone was trying to take away my responsibility to care for my little sister. If I was not there to protect her, why was I there? If I wasn't meant to look after her, how should I spend my time?

The opportunity I found in care which developed that positive focus was to become a cadet in the Air Training Corp. Eventually I succeeded in obtaining the Non-Commissioned Officer rank of Corporal. I had never heard of the ATC before foster care, and I was really hesitant about starting. It massively pushed me outside of my comfort zone, but I loved it. There was so much camaraderie, so many things to do, and I adored the discipline and the certainty of it all. I lost myself in the hiking or shooting a rifle on the range. I loved flying in a glider and losing myself in the clouds. Canoeing, camping, drill and sports. Then there was the learning. I could absorb so much about things that were never taught in school. Beyond all these passions and opportunities ATC gave me two things I will never forget.

ATC was the only place I didn't feel like a foster child. In school I was a foster child, at home I was a foster child, with my mates I was a foster child. Somehow in ATC I was just a cadet. I was treated exactly the same as everyone else. I was held to the same standard, had the same expectations, pushed the same way everyone was. I loved that space for giving me the opportunity to just be me.

The other thing ATC gave me was a belief I could do things I never thought possible. The first time I took hold of the controls of a glider, the first time I cleared a round jammed in my rifle, the occasion I went with a group of total strangers to play hockey for the Welsh wing. ATC taught me so many times that I might be afraid, but I could still move forward. For a child finding a passion, one which challenges them and nurtures them in equal measure, is so important. Here are some tips to help them find their thing.

5.1 Overcoming Insecurity and Self-Doubt

Many foster children suffer with a lack of confidence or belief. Even those who on the surface appear robust and determined can be hiding a deeper lack of worth. I was one of those children. One who even to this day the world hails as confident and extrovert but has never really felt that way. I just learnt to feel the fear and do it anyway. I have met many foster children over the years and one thing I have always found true: the loudest and seemingly most confident foster children are often the most afraid and vulnerable.

Many foster children will have experienced neglect, abuse or separation from family. All things which will have dented their confidence or sense of belonging. Here are some of the ways to help them build a sense of self-worth.

- **Success is in the little things:** Recognise successes big or small. Celebrate with them when they achieve something tricky. Sometimes that can be a huge thing, such as completing a qualification. Sometimes it may be something seemingly small like communicating their needs. Saying it out loud helps them to notice when they have achieved something. It can also help to remind them of similar achievements if they are struggling with a task.

- **The power of words:** Positive affirmations have been really helpful to me over the years. Simply telling myself over and over, "I can do this. I have what I need." Even if I get it wrong, I will learn and try again. However I find positive affirmations only feel right in certain circumstances. Sometimes trying to force the self-belief makes it harder to sustain. Finding affirmations which feel right to the child and using them when it feels right is key. Don't try to force them to believe in something out of their reach. It is more about reminding them of what they do believe they have.

- **Challenge negative thoughts:** Help them identify and reframe negative self-beliefs into more realistic and positive ones. Ask them what they are thinking, explore whether that thought is justified and if they would think that about someone else. Help them consider the perspective they are holding which is creating that idea.

- **Pride is power:** Celebrating achievements is something I am still working on. I often shy away from what feels like a fuss or even just treating myself. I am trying to find ways to do this more because I recognise how much my children enjoy me taking them out for a meal to celebrate a good school report or putting a photo up on the wall to remember their first time on the stage. Such actions can create something beyond the pleasure of a moment of celebration, something which elevates the achievement you are celebrating.

- **Service of others:** One of the biggest actions I have been able to take to build my self-worth is to give back. To be able to find ways to help others and see the direct impact. It is more impactful than the times I have raised money. Finding conversations or using my skills and work experience to help has given me a greater sense of self-worth than all the certificates I have ever been awarded and all the positive affirmations I have uttered.

5.2 Exposure and Exploration

Allow your foster children to experiment and explore different options without pressure. It's okay if they lose interest in something after a while. Finding a passion often involves trying and discarding various possibilities. Though it is important to balance this with building some staying power.

- **Let them try different things:** Let them get involved with different things, ideally not all at once but exploring the array of opportunities which exist. Encourage them to try things they may have never considered before. Sometimes we can find our happiness in the most unexpected of places. It is our role to provide varied experiences which enable the child to discover what they enjoy.
- **Ideas are often unexpected:** Don't just expose them to potential new passions through clubs. Take them to museums, historical sites or cultural events to spark curios-

ity. Expose them to the world which many of us take for granted.

- **We are often drawn to the familiar**: Don't be surprised if you face a little resistance at times. We are all inclined to seek the safety of our comfort zone. I think the comfort zone should actually be renamed to be the 'known zone'. I know I have sat in a space which is far from comfortable but well known and I have been unable to move out of it for fear of the unknown. Help them learn that as they stretch their belief, they can step outside of the things they know and they will learn more.

- **Share your passion:** Encourage them to explore hobbies you enjoy, or even introduce them to your own past passions. When my foster mum taught me to cross stich it was never something I wanted to try, and those first few basic messy animals were terrible attempts. I can't say I ever really loved cross stich, but I took something more than learning to use a needle from those moments sat together with thread. The greatest pleasure was in a shared activity.

- **Investment in their passion:** If they show interest in a particular activity, invest in some basic materials or equipment to get them started (e.g. musical instruments, art supplies, sports equipment). Investing in tools does much more than help them develop skills or get more involved, it is a tangible action which shows your investment in them and their future.

- **Think of other supports:** Resources aren't always items and sometimes can come at no cost. Look for free or low-cost resources like library programs, online tutorials or community workshops. Sometimes the greatest thing you can give them is time. Your time helping them navigate those first few steps into a new space can establish their confidence to move forward.

- **Effort is the achievement**: Recognise their hard work, dedication, and willingness to try new things, even if they don't excel right away. It is often hard for us to recognise that true success is in the steep uphill struggle and reaching the summit is just the final step. If you can focus on their courage and effort in trying new things or sticking with a practice you can build a desire to try.

- **It really is the taking part which counts:** Focus on the joy of participation and learning new skills. Talk to them afterwards about what they enjoyed or learnt. Marvel at the opportunity for them to teach you something as they grow in their knowledge and abilities.

5.3 Building Staying Power

- **Encourage them to see it through:** Discuss the importance of perseverance and sticking with something to see improvement. Offer them examples of when you have stuck with something and seen it through. Ask them to explore the feelings before and after engaging in an activity. Remind them of occasions they have not wanted to do something but have found afterwards they were really happy they did.

- In our home we have an expectation that if the girls have committed to attending something and then decide they don't want to go, they have to attend that session and then afterwards we discuss if they still don't want to go back. A number of times our youngest has said she does not want to go horse riding only to return home with a noticeable buzz of delight. Though there have been occasions like with Rainbows when she went twice and consistently said she did not want to go back, so we let her decide to stop attending.
- Be understanding if they face challenges, but gently nudge them to keep trying. If there is regular desire to stop an activity be supportive. Perhaps give them some time before trying something new. For most children the biggest challenge to overcome when trying something new is fear. Remind them that without fear there is no courage.

- **Break down the goal:** Help them set realistic goals and celebrate milestones along the way. If everyone around them is working towards bigger goals figure out what feels right for them. Likewise don't underestimate them, and make sure the goals you set are challenging enough to spark their development and growth.

- **Be their biggest cheerleader:** Show genuine interest in their activities, attend their games or performances, and listen to them talk about their experiences. Even if they have taken up a passion which does not interest you, remember it is not about you becoming an expert in that thing. It is about you becoming an expert in the child and learning about them.

- **Tell everyone about their amazing attributes:** My mother was my biggest cheerleader. From a distance and often not there in those moments I needed her most, but somehow that sense of belief was there. I remember nervously standing at the side of the stage the first time I was going to sing a solo. She was not in the audience, but she was who I thought about cheering me on. Whoever my mother met she would tell them how wonderful I was. I didn't need to hear it myself although I occasionally did. Somehow simply based on the fanfare my mother created in my wake there would be a sense of wonder in others of who I was. I could feel that. Having that one person you know believes in you is priceless. If you can't find one thing you admire in a child, look harder.

5.4 Summary

Finding a passion is a journey, not a destination. It takes time, patience, and a supportive environment. The most important thing is to create a safe space where the child feels comfortable exploring their interests and expressing themselves. Interests might change over time or as they grow. Some children may hold multiple interests and others only one. When a child wants to share a passion with you, put down your phone and give them your full attention. How they feel about something is often influenced by how others respond. Listening intently to them will help you understand their interests and build their commitment. The value of taking the time to help them discover their passion goes beyond giving them a focus or something to enjoy. It can empower them to continue to explore and grow for the rest of their lives.

CHAPTER 6

Show Up

I was highly independent as a child. You would probably expect that given all I had been through. Before I was ten years old not only was I cooking tea for my little sister and me, helping her get ready for school, or washed or dressed, I was also helping to manage my mother's complex mental health issues, communicating my needs to professionals and advocating for my little sister and me. I think sometimes when all the pressure of looking after my little sister was taken away and I was placed in a safe environment people seemed almost surprised that the extreme independence didn't just melt away. That I didn't overnight just settle back into being a carefree child.

I don't think this is actually a transition any of us can make easily. It feels akin to asking Adam after eating the apple to forget everything he now knows. If you are working with a child who is persistently pushing away your support or insisting they don't need you, please show up anyway. You can always sit outside the room or at the back of the school hall. Being there consistently gives them the opportunity to trust you will be there when they need you.

There were many occasions I remember no one being there for me when I really needed them. When I was still small, I had my tonsils removed after repeated infections and being very poorly. As I came around from the surgery I looked for someone I knew, and no one was there. All I found was a pot of flowers next to my bed with a note from my mum. This was the closest she could be. She was sectioned in a mental health hospital. No one else came. It wasn't the only time I found myself alone in a hospital. In high school I had been playing hockey and managed to get my head cracked open with a hockey stick. My teacher was very apologetic that she had to leave me, but she had a minibus full of children outside. The hospital called my father. I assume he was still written down as my emergency contact. My dad said that he would come and get me after EastEnders finished. I sat alone on a chair in the ward in silence whilst they fixed up my head and waited for over an hour for anyone to come and deposit me back at my foster parents' house. These experiences, while seemingly minor, reinforced a deep sense of isolation.

The challenge for many children in care is that the people in their lives are fluid and inconsistent. From social workers and family members to medical professionals and teachers. Sometimes the outcome of these ever-changing supports is harder to manage than always being alone. The lack of certainty drives an almost constant fear that support might get taken away, often producing an extreme independence which is not healthy.

I have heard social workers proudly refer to the children they support as independent. This can quickly become a risk for the child if they are praised constantly for standing on their own two feet and getting on with stuff alone.

The cost of learning independence at such a young age goes far beyond those moments when you had to stop being a child and act as the adult you needed. It can create an inability to ask for help. A lack of trust in others. A fear of losing the love you desperately need, so much so that you push it away rather than having to risk learning again what that pain feels like. Here are some ways you can show up and build that sense of trust.

6.1 Communication is Key

In care I never had that one person I could speak to. Despite all the wonderful relationships around me each of them carried a reason I could not open up. Be it fear of a backlash. A desire to protect them. A fear of the consequences. The main reason which meant I never communicated my emotions was simply my fear of the feelings. I had seen my mother overwhelmed by emotions so many times. I remember watching hours of Star Trek and trying my best to be more like Spock. To force logic into all of my actions. Now I always try to build open and varied channels of communication with my girls. I hope that if they ever needed someone, they would know I am always there ready to listen. Here are some ways communication helped or may have been helpful in my care.

- **Actively listen to them:** When they talk to you repeat to them what they say to confirm you have understood. Don't assume the meaning or intent behind what they are saying or how they are saying it. It is possible they have not had the best role models to learn from. Ask them "Is your goal to hurt my feelings?" If the answer is yes, ask why. Often though the answer will be no and they are just communicating poorly. If they open up to about anything, maybe something that happened in school or perhaps something more upsetting, if it feels appropriate gently ask questions, reassuring them they don't have to talk about it but you are there if they need to. Asking questions shows you care, and importantly for a child who may have struggled with traumatic situations, shows you are not scared and can create a safe space.

- **Phone calls:** Encourage the people supporting them to schedule regular phone calls or video chats, even if it's just for a short check-in. Consistency is key, so stick to a set schedule whenever possible. My mum would always call to speak with me on a Sunday evening. Knowing that call would always come built a rhythm and trust even though she could not be there.

- **Appointment support**: If you can't attend an appointment with the child, explain why beforehand and offer to call them during or after. Talk them through what might happen at the appointment and check if they feel they need any help. Ask them for updates on how it went. I remember all the extra appointments. Doctor's check-ups, social worker reviews. Somehow it made me feel like I was on a factory line and the adults were lining me up to inspect and tick a box. Helping a child navigate these sessions and focusing on the purpose to ensure they are cared for can provide a better experience.

- **Leave notes and messages:** Leave handwritten notes or record short video messages expressing your care and support. With my girls I love nothing more than slipping the occasional note in their lunch box. When they are facing a really hard day like the first day of school, I tie a little ribbon and slip it in their coat pocket or draw a small heart on the sleeve of their top. That way they can pop their hand in the pocket and feel the object there or look at the heart and know I am thinking of them.

- **Utilise technology:** Explore communication options like texting or using co-parenting apps to stay connected and share updates throughout the day. With my eldest we have a family WhatsApp group. The important messages go there and that way we all get to see them and give support. It helps my husband out too as he often forgets when exams are or if our eldest is out for tea. She also loves the occasional gif or emoji rather than words which can feel hard to articulate.

A word of caution on the tech. We use tracking devices in our family, but they are a shared tool, and we are open about their use. When she went on a school trip to another country I also gave her an extra Apple tag to wear. I would never use anything like that without her consent or it would hugely damage the trust. We also agreed before she went what the plan was with daily calls or texting. We agreed that I would try to call her once in the morning and then leave her to enjoy the day. Having open conversations about expectations helped her find a level of freedom and support which worked.

• **Let the child lead:** Try various approaches for communication. Be open to trying new things which may not be your natural instinct. Any child knows themselves best and will often lead you to the best forms of communication for them.

6.2 Building a Support Network

It takes a village. When I reflect on modern parenting even outside of the spaces of children in care I realise we have lost so much of our community mentality. The most common narrative is one that we should not put upon others. That we are not performing as parents unless we are cracking on alone. It was not so long ago that the street would all be involved in helping to look out for a child. Or that families would adopt 'aunties' and 'uncles' like a circus troupe. We have forgotten that when we ask for help we are not only admitting we need support, we are allowing someone else the opportunity to be there for us. Supporting one another is the greatest gift we can give in life. For children in care this village approach is more important as they navigate additional challenges and can find their support structure frequently changing. Here are some things to consider when recruiting for your village.

- **Involve the child:** When building a support network, involve the child in the process as much as possible. Let them know who these people are and how they can be reached. Ask the child who is in their village. We have a support network around our girls which includes people they know would be there in an emergency to people who can help with studies or questions. Talking to the child about who they would like to support them can identify opportunities to extend the relationships they have. I really missed out not only on the relationships with my brothers but with other people who had been in my life before care, and I lost contact with during my time in care.

- **Connect with teachers and caregivers**: Maintain regular communication with teachers, therapists or other caregivers involved in the child's life. This shows a unified front and demonstrates your commitment to their wellbeing. We always talk about school reports together and I always discuss with my eldest before I email the school. I think this is important to ensure she knows it's us against the world and not us adults against her. If I have a concern or want to speak to her teachers, she helps me shape the narrative and I keep her informed of the conversation.

- **Extended family and friends:** If appropriate, facilitate connections with trusted extended family or friends who can offer additional support and stability. When I was in foster care I found so much happiness in seeing the relationships in the family. Getting to meet the aunts and uncles. The boys, my foster parents' biological sons, were wonderful. I lost contact with most of my extended family and my other siblings when I was in care. Seeing examples of trusting relationships can help the child build their own.

- **Be okay with someone else stepping up:** I remember with our youngest her dad stayed at home with her, and I went back to work. This inevitably meant he could often understand what she was saying better than me and for a time she would go to him for help first. I had to learn not to feel a sense of rejection or that I was failing her. I knew logically she spent more time with him, but it was easy to feel a little upset. When you build a village, you need to be okay with the child leaning into others and perhaps not coming to you. Recognise you are succeeding when you create a network of support and the confidence to ask for it. And that all parents have times when their child chooses not to engage with them.

6.3 Actions Speak Louder Than Words

I remember the day I walked into my mother's bedroom. As she sat on her flowery bedsheets, she took her hands in mine and told me, "It is going to be okay. I have thrown away all my razor blades."

I was still in primary school. Still living at home. As she smiled through her tears with hope in her eyes, I didn't have the heart to tell her I knew that would not be the case. I heard many promises made by family, by social workers, by friends. Many wishes they had, they wanted to do these things, but they often failed to deliver. As a child in care I gave up believing in the promises. Perhaps it made me even more grateful when they did arrive. For children in care words often hold little weight. Reflecting on the importance of actions helps build a sense of trust.

- **Follow through on commitments:** Always keep your promises, big or small. If something unexpected comes up and you can't make it, explain beforehand and reschedule as soon as possible. Be aware that sometimes for a foster child the small examples of going back on your word can have a huge impact. Even little things like if you say there will be a certain meal for dinner and you change your mind. For a child who may have experienced huge failings any small ones are like warning smoke. They can quickly decide if you can go back on that what else will you fail to follow through on?
- **Be reliable:** Be someone the child can count on to be there for them emotionally, even if you can't be physically present. Managing your own emotions but not hiding them is important. It is hard to build a sense of

connection and trust if the person you are connecting with is not available and open. I could absolutely tell when the adults around me were holding something back. I think as a child who grew up reading a room before anyone uttered a word it was hard to hide anything from me. I learnt quickly that people rarely say how they feel. This only taught me to keep my feelings locked away too.

- **Respect their boundaries**: Respect their need for space and privacy. Don't be pushy, but always let them know you're available if they need you. If they insist they don't need your support, but you sense they really could benefit from it, step away short term. You can still offer it again further down the line. I was wonderful at helping. Awful at asking for help. I was afraid that if I became too familiar, relying on others, then when I lost that support I would fail. It was better to be okay with standing on my own feet than risk finding myself unexpectedly alone.

6.4 Building Trust Takes Time

I learnt to trust my foster parents absolutely. Their consistency in approach. The way they would follow through on actions and commitments. I found a sense of stability and connection I never expected to have. Though this trust was not easily won, I recognise the effort they put in to give me that steadiness. When building a relationship with a child in care it is worth being kind to yourself and considering the following.

Be patient: Building trust takes time and consistent effort. Don't get discouraged if a child seems closed off at first, or if you face a setback. No development is ever a straight line to the goal, and we all make mistakes. The key is to stick with it. In my case files there are notes the social worker has written stating my foster mum certainly felt frozen out at times. You can see though how over time I settled a little more not only into the home but into those relationships.

Be understanding: Remember, their past experiences may make them hesitant to trust easily. Remember you bring your own experiences, wants and abilities. It is understandable you might get frustrated when you are only trying to help, or you keep getting pushed away. It is probably not about you and more about the child and their challenges. Have patience and you will get there.

Be a safe space: Create a safe space where they feel comfortable expressing their emotions and needs without judgement. For instance, not shutting a conversation down when it gets hard. Always being available when they need you, or if you can't, create a space soon after. I found that safe space in my foster sister. She was a wonderful friend, confidant and a bit of a protector. At least I felt she would protect me.

6.5 Summary

Whilst we work to be there for a child it is also important to still nurture their independence and skills. Foster children will often need to advocate for themselves and act more independently than the average child. For many foster children when they leave the care system they may find themselves back in a position of extremely limited, if any, support. Think about the skills you can nurture now which will benefit them in the future. Anything from helping them to learn to cook, ride a bike or deal with conflict. Practical, emotional and social skills are all important skills for them to master.

Showing up consistently is sometimes harder than you would think. Life often throws us curve balls. It is important to achieve this goal as much as possible and be understanding on the occasions you just can't. Having someone show up for you says more than "I care", or "I want to support you". It says "You are not alone". It says "You are worth persisting for". It says "You might never need help but if you do it is there". It may take time for a child to learn they can rely on someone. Please don't give up on them. By consistently showing up in these ways, foster parents and social workers can demonstrate their commitment to the child's wellbeing and build a foundation of trust that will last.

CHAPTER 7

It's Not About the Gifts

If you asked me what my favourite gift was as a child, I couldn't tell you. I remember one doll I played with for years and a teddy with a patch on his leg, but I don't remember when they were given to me. As a foster child I valued relationships more than material gifts. However fostering these connections proved challenging, especially with the frequent transitions and separations inherent in the foster care system. Going into care I lost many of my existing relationships, and the same thing happened when I left. Losing those connections twice in my life was extremely challenging. It was like finding myself in a foreign land with no one to help translate. I didn't understand them, they didn't understand me. We had lost that shared time growing up which creates an understanding of who we are as individuals. Supporting continued relationships is not always easy. As foster children, we have a diverse support network and must navigate the complexities of professional relationships from a young age. Based on my own experiences and the stories of others, here are some practical tips for fostering these crucial connections.

7.1 Relationships with Biological Family

Throughout my time in care I may have seen my elder brothers only once. The focus of social services was in maintaining contact with my parents, but these relationships were the most damaging I experienced. My elder brothers didn't go into care, and I understand the many reasons they stepped back from our world when they had the chance. Still, I wish things had been different. I once asked if I could see more of my brothers. To this day I don't know if anyone tried to connect with them or if that request was lost. I was able to reconnect with them years after I left care, but there are gaps in our understanding of each other.

My mother was the relative I held the strongest relationship with. It was complex as she was not allowed to know where we lived. We would only meet with her a handful of times a year. There would often be occasions when a meeting with mum was cancelled. Nothing could prepare me for the disappointment and worry which followed. I knew this meant suicide attempts and self-harm. It was a conflicting and difficult relationship to navigate. I would long for that time with her and fear it in equal measure.

Whilst navigating these relationships was challenging at times, I wish I had the opportunity to have more contact with members of my wider family. This difficulty in maintaining contact with my biological family is a common challenge faced by many foster children. Reflecting on the challenges of maintaining contact with my family, I realised how crucial it is for foster children to have continued positive relationships. Here are some strategies to help maintain those vital family connections.

- **The value of family relationships:** It is vital to acknowledge the importance of biological family ties, even if the relationship is strained. For all the difficulties I found in maintaining a relationship with my mother I still look back on her letters and find love and connection in her words. It can feel difficult to manage, but allowing a child to maintain a relationship with family teaches life skills well beyond the value of holding a connection.
- **Be mindful of the impact:** Be aware of any ongoing negative impact on the child and ensure that, overall, they are benefiting from the relationship. I speak with foster children regularly who maintain contact out of a sense of responsibility, and when they describe the occasions they speak or meet with a relative, they struggle to find any examples of feeling good or a positive interaction. If this becomes apparent explore the decision to maintain contact.
- **Safe connection:** Work with social workers to facilitate safe and supervised contact. There may be a number of requirements placed on contact. Sometimes the timing,

setting and attendees are fixed. Dependent on the child and circumstances this can create frustration and confusion as they don't understand or see the level of risk which is being managed.

When we visited mum it would most often be in the high security hospital, in staged family rooms with locked doors and tense supervisors. I would find myself surveying the room for dangers and sitting on the edge of my seat ready to escape or defend myself. Try to find ways to make contact productive. Giving a focus to the contact, like reviewing a school report together or playing a game can be helpful.

- **Be emotionally prepared:** Help the child understand why contact may be limited and prepare them for potential emotional responses. Talk to them in advance about what contact might be like and the realities that mean it may not happen.
- **Don't force it:** Be as flexible as you can, and if there is a cancellation try to rearrange contact as soon as possible. Equally, try not to apply pressure on the child. If they don't want to have contact on an occasion it is important to try to support them. If they persistently don't want contact it is worth exploring why, but don't force it.
- **Consider including family:** If appropriate and where possible consider including the child's extended family in celebrations or informal get togethers. Keeping at-

tachments alive where safe to do so will help a child build trust and sustainable relationships with family and carers.

7.2 Relationships with Foster Siblings

On my first day in care, my foster sister walked through the hallway while I sat in silence. The look she gave me could have scared even the most resilient person. I thought that was it – I had no chance of surviving this. I was a competent, outspoken child but I was not hard by any means. I could tell she was tough, and the social worker had already warned me she had cracked another child's head open with a metal talcum powder tin. Unbelievably, we discovered our birthday was on exactly the same day, and she was one year older than me. Since that moment we were inseparable. I grew up admiring and loving her like she was the big sister I always wanted. I always felt safest when I was with her. Foster children may not always get along but if you can nurture relationships within the home they may find companions for life. To help develop those connections you can think about:

- **Shared experiences and activities:** To nurture relationships between foster children you can create shared activities and routines to foster a sense of family and belonging. Even shared time watching television or encouraging board games. My foster sister and I would spend hours playing cards or Labyrinth.

- **Encourage cooperation and communication between siblings:** Help foster siblings navigate potential conflicts and teach healthy ways to resolve disagreements. Try not to set children against each other. If they are struggling avoid picking a side. Support them both to articulate to each other how they are feeling and why they are feeling that way. It can be helpful to focus apologies on actions. If someone got hurt encourage the other child to help them with a cold compress, or if something was broken help them fix it.

7.3 Relationships with Other Children

All the way through primary school I had a close-knit group of amazing friends. Then when I went into foster care we drifted. So much so that I stopped speaking with them. To this day I don't know what created that division. Did I pull away or did they drift? I know that once I went into care my school friends never really came to my foster home. I think the reality is that their parents weren't happy with them coming to play there. I also often felt like I wanted to keep those things separate. I wish my friendships had been more stable. To this day I wish I had held on to that group of childhood friends.

Friendships can be especially challenging for foster children as they navigate relocations and school changes. To support foster children in preserving these vital connections, consider the following strategies.

- **Building a parenting network:** It can help for you to build a connection with the parents of your foster children's friends. Perhaps arrange a group activity where the parents can meet you as well. There are still many incorrect negative perspectives of children in care, and you may need to help break down this stigma. Building relationships yourself can help to create a space where the child's friendships can thrive.

- **Clubs and connections**: Help the child participate in extracurricular activities or clubs to meet like-minded peers. Help them build a network of people with shared interests as a way to establish connections.

- **Learning what good friendships look like:** Encourage open communication and offer guidance on building healthy friendships. Be mindful that the child may fall into unhealthy relationships; they may need help to recognise and navigate this. It is not about picking their friends for them but about helping them recognise and engage in positive relationships. They may need help learning how to build boundaries when needed.

- **Navigating friendship milestones:** Simple friendship milestones like the first unaccompanied playdate or a sleepover can be really complex for a child in care to navigate. There are often many requirements placed on carers to ensure the safety and wellbeing of a child. These can mean usual activities become complex or not possible. Anticipating these types of requests and understanding in advance what the requirements may be is important. Helping the child to understand and navigate these opportunities in a proactive way means that you can avoid the situation where a child agrees to something and then has to back out. Try to find ways to foster a normal friendship or activities with friends. If barriers do arise consider compromises such as allowing the child to stay at a friend's as late as possible then picking them up just before the other children go to sleep.

7.4 Relationships with Foster Parents

I was close to my foster parents. Of course we had our disagreements. For all the ways I was wonderful as a child I was also stubborn beyond measure. I can imagine at times this mix of headstrong and immovable was hard work. I know at times my anger at the world and life could spill into a day. My foster mum was always really patient and took everything in her stride. She didn't get ruffled easily, and I think she knew that even when I was being difficult, it was never about her.

Some of my favourite memories were simply things like Sunday afternoon sandwiches and cake. Or when my foster dad would take me for a ride on his motorbike. I remember the one day he was taking me to an airshow and the bike broke down. We spent hours sat in a field talking, feeding a horse nearby and watching the planes in the far-off distance. It was wonderful. Funny how sometimes those memories which are most enjoyable were when things didn't go to plan. They peppered my life with little moments of pure joy, and I will be eternally grateful for that.

When I left care I lost all contact with them. I found myself back in worsening abuse, and as my world collapsed around me I didn't feel I could reach out. I do wonder sometimes if they had tried to stay in touch, would they have noticed how bad things were getting and been able to help. After escaping my father's home and settling on my own, I reached out and rebuilt our relationship. In those later years they showed me more kindness again. My foster father taught me to drive a car. It was the proudest day of my life when I graduated with a distinction and they both came to see me. Building a relationship with a child, whether it ends when they leave care or continues throughout their lives, helps establish trust and love. Building such bonds can be incredibly rewarding for both foster children and parents. Here are some things to remember to develop a strong, supportive relationship.

- **Quality not quantity:** Spend quality time together, one-on-one and as a family. There is a huge amount of pressure to spend time with our children. Recognise this pressure and try not to build overwhelming expectations of how much time you spend together. This can vary hugely from child to child, dependent on age, personality, time of the year and many other factors. What is important is when you spend time together it is quality time. Put away distractions like mobile phones. Engage in something fun or constructive. Create a variety of opportunities from sitting quietly together to going out and engaging in a shared hobby or passion.

- **Relationships take time:** Be patient, understanding, and create a safe space for open communication. Always remember, like most children who are still learning to manage their emotions, foster children are often faced with more trauma to navigate and less understanding of how to do so. Role modelling, respect and compassion can help build a mutual care for each other over time.
- **Long-term connection:** If you can maintain a relationship with the child it can be hugely beneficial. This relationship can take whatever form you would like. Perhaps you might continue to send a birthday card each year. Or maybe you are able to have regular contact. If a child goes on to another placement or ages out (leaves social care support) don't assume they want nothing more to do with you. Even strained relationships can be hard to lose. Build a relationship which feels right for both of you. Accept this may vary for each child or each period of their life.

Being in care presents a unique reality for relationships, often marked by abrupt endings and a sense of loss. It's crucial to find ways to build and sustain long-term connections which can provide much-needed stability and support. Whilst you are in care your foster family, residential team, social workers and anyone else supporting you want to invest in building a relationship with you, but when you leave all this disappears. Some foster parents are told not to maintain relationships after care. Social workers are often encouraged to establish firm boundaries and cut off communication once the child has left care. When there is a forced hard break in these relationships it somehow makes it feel like none of it was real to begin with. It can be extra damaging and heartbreaking to feel a continued or repeated sense of abandonment.

7.5 Summary

It is worth touching briefly on giving and receiving gifts. Gifting carries a greater significance than simply a celebration. A gift expresses the value you place upon the child, your love for them, the kindness of another, and your worth in being able to offer something to them. Gift giving for foster children can be complex. The multiple relationships they manage. The financial constraints, especially if you care for many children. The challenges of expectation meeting reality. These are some important considerations when gift giving to a foster child.

- **Don't overwhelm:** Consider the previous experiences of the child. Try not to overwhelm them; they may not have received lots of presents before. Perhaps give them time to open presents at Christmas over the course of the day. Go at their pace.
- **Avoid second-hand:** If you can, avoid second hand gifts for a foster child. It is likely they may have already struggled with self-worth and a second-hand gift can be received as a message they are worth less. Of course, if you always buy second-hand or if there is a financial

need to purchase second-hand do so, but be clear with the child your reason for this.

- **The personal touch:** A thoughtful gift can have far greater value. You could make a card or give them a homemade present. Consider buying them an experience or taking them out to create a memory. Be curious about what they like, keep notes of things they mention throughout the year. The time and effort to consider what is the best gift for each individual child can provide more joy than a spontaneous purchase.
- **Help them gift too:** Understand if there are people, they would like to buy gifts for. I always remember in school when my friends would exchange presents at Christmas and my paper round money could never stretch very far, I felt awful turning up with the little I could muster.

Whilst gift giving is a core component of our lives, I continue to value my relationships far beyond the receiving of a gift. I am grateful now for all the wonderful people in my life and continue to learn how to build healthy boundaries and connections. These lessons underscore the importance of nurturing relationships for foster children, helping them to develop a strong, supportive network that can guide them throughout their lives.

CHAPTER 8

I Need to Be Heard

As children many of us wish we had more of a say. We want to be heard. To feel grown up and to get our way. As a child who experienced horrific abuse, I learnt to be silent. All I heard even from those who loved me was, "We don't talk about that", "Not now", "Not here". I quickly understood that the things I wanted to say were wrong. I interpreted that in the only way most children would, that I was wrong. So I learnt to be silent. Of course I spoke like most other children, but I never really said any of the things which needed to be said. I locked them away in that place with no escape. They echoed through my mind. A constant dialogue of pain, disgust, confusion and loss. At some points in my life I didn't even have the language to articulate what I was experiencing.

To support the children we care for it is important to remain curious and observant. To notice the little things which are said or not said. To recognise the ways beyond words that a child may try to communicate. Silence, aggression or defiance are all forms of communication. By continually being inquisitive about a child's experiences and the way they may express or fail to express their emotions we can be open to helping them learn. To develop their own skills in connecting with and mastering their methods of communication.

I remember the occasions when I negotiated my way into protection meetings or reviews of my care. It was the most unnerving experience to sit in a room and hear everyone speak about me in the third person, as if I wasn't there. Worse still was the way they spoke about my life and the things I had experienced with such cold specificity. As if dealing with an order for one abused child action plan with a side of protection. There were many occasions when I needed someone to hear me, to believe me and to advocate for me.

Advocating for a child does not always mean you have to agree with them. You are helping them to be heard in a room full of adults who can easily drown them out. Helping them find the words to express how they feel and what they need. Creating a safe space for communication and teaching them how to advocate for themselves instils lifelong skills. From understanding how they feel, communicating their needs and learning to advocate, here are some approaches to develop the skills they need.

8.1 Role modelling communication

The best way to learn is often from seeing examples of how to do it well before practising yourself. Many children in care will have failed to have a good role model to learn from. Simple communication methods like eye contact and volume may be underdeveloped. When communicating with children in care we can also find the topic of conversation is more difficult to navigate. Here are some ways you can role model the best approaches to communication.

- **Emphasise active listening:** Put away distractions, make eye contact, and truly listen to what the child is saying, both verbally and nonverbally. Children will often find what feels like the most inconvenient times to open up. Just before bed is a classic as they reflect on the day and perhaps find themselves afraid to go to sleep. I often found myself afraid of sleep because I couldn't escape the nightmares.

Another time I would often want to chat to my foster mum was whilst she was busy cooking in the kitchen. I don't know if that was because I spent my first few hours in their home there, or because she would often be happy when she was cooking. Whenever a child opens up try to put down the chores or delay bedtime for ten minutes. They may not have the courage to open up again.

- **Acknowledge the situation:** Don't minimise their experiences. Acknowledge their pain, fear or anger without judgement. The first time my therapist said "I am sorry you experienced that." the words hit me like a bus. It wasn't his fault. He hadn't known me as a child and yet as the words sunk in, I realised how much I had needed to hear that. I needed someone to sit with me and recognise how hard it had been. To acknowledge that it was awful and just like me on some level wish it had not happened.

- **Validate their feelings:** For some an apology can feel empty, or patronising. They value more the recognition of what they are feeling. Saying things like "I can see you are struggling with this." Or "That must feel like crap." helps them feel seen and understood. You don't need to understand the reason why they may be feeling the way they are. Sometimes it won't make sense but that's okay. Recognising their feelings whatever they are can help them move forward.

- **Use "I" statements:** Before foster care I always felt I had to walk on eggshells, that anything I might do could be wrong. The fear of those words "You upset your mother" or "You made your dad angry". Those accusations were thrown at me time and again, often pre-empting a period when my mother would get sick and try to harm herself or an occasion when my father would become angry or abusive. I grew up hyper aware of the impact my words and behaviour could have. This resulted in so much self-hatred throughout my life. If you need to challenge a behaviour because of the impact it is having, instead of accusatory statements, like "You should tell me how you feel" use "I" statements to communicate your feelings about their behaviour. For example, "I feel worried when you withdraw and don't talk to me."

8.2 Encouraging Expression Through Various Means

Over the years when I talk about my past experiences, I receive a variety of responses. From shock and horror to people wanting to shut down the conversation or asking a hundred detailed questions. I am still learning how to process these conversations. I have learnt to build boundaries and politely decline if the conversation gets too difficult. I have learnt that those shutting it down are not trying to shut me down but protect themselves from the upset of hearing what are difficult things to hear. The hardest response I struggle to process is shock or horror. That look of disgust on someone's face feels like it is directed at me. The inbuilt shame is a hard shackle to free myself from, and talking to others does not always feel safe. Here are some ways to help children communicate their feelings.

- **Offer alternative communication methods:** Not everyone feels comfortable expressing themselves verbally. When I was young I don't think I even had the right language. Providing options like writing, drawing or playing can help them communicate their feelings. For me poetry became a release that I rarely shared with anyone but found great solace in. I could lose myself in those pages, the ink bleeding out my rage, fear and sometimes hope. I loved that poetry felt like it didn't have to make sense, that it could convey a feeling or tell a story without ever explaining the detail of a memory I would rather leave behind.

- **Prepare them for the response:** Discussing with them the reactions they may receive or have experienced helps lessen their impact. Exploring what might sit behind that response can help them recognise it is more about the person reacting and not about them.

8.3 Responding to Trauma and Abuse

When communicating with a child in care there is a greater chance they will open up about trauma or abuse. These can be difficult things to hear about. I know from my own experiences whilst they are hard to hear they are even harder to talk about. It is important if a child takes the opportunity to talk about their experiences, we create a space which helps them to continue communicating. In my experience the following considerations have helped when in this situation.

- **Listen intently:** Stop what you are doing and give them your full attention. If you find they are struggling to talk it can help to go for a walk. There is something about being side by side and having a focus other than the conversation which can help alleviate the pressure. I often remember when I was simply peeling potatoes or tidying a room I felt most at ease to discuss some of the harder topics.

- **Ask questions:** It is okay to gently ask clarifying questions. Let them know it is okay if they don't want to answer. I find it really helpful when people ask me questions about my experiences. It lets me know they are okay to talk about it and the question can help frame a messy and confusing past.

- **Accept what they say and take it seriously:** The absolute majority of the time the experience they are sharing is very real for them. Regardless of whether they have accurately recalled the whole event, accept what they are telling you. The damage done by not believing them far outweighs the impact of treading down a path and discovering it is the wrong road to take.

- **Use age-appropriate language:** Tailor your communication style to the child's age and level of understanding. If you are not sure of their understanding let them lead the conversation. If they use words or phrases which you are not sure they understand, gently ask what they think they mean.

- **Our experiences are unique:** Remember we all experience the world through our own set of filters. If their experience doesn't match with what you know it doesn't mean it is untrue. A child's perspective can be very different. At times their memory may even adjust the recollection of events to protect them from the impact of trauma.

8.4 Empower Self-Advocacy

- **Prepare them for meetings:** Talk to them about who might be at a meeting, what the agenda might be. Practice scenarios like care reviews or therapy sessions together. Help them anticipate questions and how to express their needs. If they know certain questions are going to be asked they might find it helpful to write down or list the key points they want to get across.
- **Help them find their voice:** Brainstorm ways they can advocate for themselves in meetings. Could they put their hand up to interject? What statements can they use to firmly articulate disagreement in a way which engages others in a conversation rather than shuts a discussion down?
- **Respect their decisions:** Allow the child to make age-appropriate choices and respect their opinions on matters affecting them. Sometimes their decisions can be confusing or not feel right to those caring for the child. Let them know if you feel a decision is not the right one and explain your reasons why, but where the decision is something they should make, respect them by supporting how they choose to move forward.

This can be a tricky space as the decisions children in care face can often be far outside the realms of a decision most children face at that age. I certainly know I made some bad decisions in my time in care. I made lots of decisions for the benefit and sake of others. I do wish someone had been more assertive in challenging my choices at times, but I recognise I was not easily influenced and was artful at negotiating the outcome I wanted. I think eventually people gave up debating with me because they recognised once I had made my mind up, I was often set on that course. I think if someone had said to me, "I don't think this is the right choice because I think you will be hurt, and you need to know it is okay if at any point you change your mind." Having that reassurance it's okay to get it wrong may have meant when I did, I would have felt more able to turn back and ask for help.

- **Help them improve their communication:** I have heard the response from social workers when a child has disclosed abuse. The most common response by far when a child discloses these things is disbelief. I understand the concerns about children being honest. Often the sense of a lack of honesty is a symptom of the child's inability to communicate effectively. They often don't have a grasp of language in the way we do, and they certainly have a number of lenses on life which colour their view of the world in all sorts of ways. Helping a child to articulate their experiences and needs clearly is important in establishing their credibility. Help them to speak clearly and with certainty.
- **Acknowledge when it is hard:** Acknowledge when a meeting or situation has been difficult. "Phew that was a tough one! They really put us through our paces. Well

done for using your voice regardless of the outcome." Recognise that they may not always get the outcome they wanted, but there is value in communicating their needs now and in the future.

8.5 Being Their Advocate

- **Amplify their voice:** It didn't happen often, but sometimes I lost my voice. I would either sit in silence dazed and confused by the debates happening around me, or I would stumble over my words failing to articulate effectively anything I wanted to say. I remember once one of my social workers turning to me in a meeting and simply asking "Is there anything you would like to add, Row?" Those words unlocked my ability to speak, and I found myself reengaged in the conversation. When the child struggles to express themselves in meetings, use your voice to advocate for their needs, but do not speak on their behalf unless they have asked you. You may be able to prompt them with a question you think might enable them to speak up or explore other methods of communication such as visuals or pre-written statements.

- **Be their translator:** Children may use nonverbal cues or behaviours to express what's wrong. As you care for a child you might notice patterns or signs they are struggling. Sometimes the cause is apparent: a cancelled visit, a difficult situation in school. Often though there might be no apparent cause. That does not mean there is not a reason for their behaviour. Help social workers or therapists understand the child's underlying emotions and the ways they are coping with the impact of those feelings.

- **Maintain open communication with professionals:** Foster parents should communicate openly with social workers and therapists about the child's needs and preferences. The importance here is that you are transparent with the child. If they share something with you and you feel it is important to communicate this with their wider support network, let them know. It is important to communicate that you are working to try and build the best possible future for them and to do that you sometimes need to talk about difficult things so everyone can support them better.

- **Never talk about them like they are not in the room:** This can be a tricky one for professionals who move between meetings and contexts. I recall the first time I sat in a meeting and the room spoke as if I was not there. The police, social workers and others were discussing a prohibitive steps order against my mother. They were talking about risks and how best to manage them and the whole conversation happened as if I was not there in the room. Sometimes they didn't even use my name. They would say things like "We are concerned there is a significant risk to the children. We are not confident that they would be safeguarded if this were to happen." There was something very 'othering' about hearing myself talked about in that way. Something dehumanising and dissociative. If you are in a setting and discussing the care of a child with them present, always, as difficult as it may be, address them or the risks towards them directly.

- **Sing their praises:** The greatest examples I have ever experienced of those advocating for me have been later in life in my professional career. I will always fondly remember the mentor who sent an email to all of his senior contacts when I told him I wanted to work in Inclusion. He created skip line meetings with directors and sang my praises far and wide. Or the charity CEO who when I told them of my ambition to be a writer, reached out to contacts asking them to support me and helping me to build that network. Or the line manager who created opportunities for me to achieve things I never thought possible and would encourage me to stretch myself beyond my comfort zone. Advocating for someone does much more than help their immediate needs be met, it builds their sense of self-belief and that is priceless.

8.6 Summary

As a child learns to communicate and advocate for themselves and others, they will establish a sense of empowerment and confidence. Helping them develop these skills across multiple settings and circumstances will enable them to have their needs meet more often. Many children in care look back on their time in care and find opportunities where they felt unheard or unseen. Giving them a voice can allow them to step into the space where they own their journey.

CHAPTER 9

I Need to Feel Loved

For years love meant never stepping out of line. Always trying to keep everyone happy. A dance of extremes from rejection and fear to warmth and comfort. At its most extreme love meant almost losing my life. There were people in my life I loved, like my mother despite all the terrible things she did to us. And there were people like my father who I feared. When we moved into care that changed. As a minimum I got to see firsthand what a normal loving relationship looked like. Sometimes I even felt a little bit of that love myself. Those examples offered me a different model to broaden my understanding of the value and importance of love.

Sadly, for all the great examples I found, even with the wonderful loving marriage I managed to find my way to, for all my life there has been one person I have failed to learn to love. Myself. I have only ever felt a deep unyielding hate towards myself. I hated myself for the things I failed to protect my mother from. I hated myself for the things I allowed to happen to my body. I hated myself for the bad decisions I made. That hatred was never confined to my past. It bled into every day. I hated the things I said, the actions I messed up. Every example adding weight to the case I was only deserving of that hate.

For children in care love is often a challenge. I have met children over the years who yearn for love so much they latch onto any sign of kindness, submerging themselves in the simple possibility of a connection. Or children who have given up on love so completely that they refuse to entertain the possibility of it. They place no value in it or see it as weakness. Love may be defined in many ways to different people. A sense of warmth, or connection or belonging. A feeling or chemical reaction. However you define love, for a child having the opportunity to experience love, seeing it role modelled, or learning to love themselves is an essential part of development. This chapter covers many ideas from how we can create a loving environment to how we can signal our love or build their self-esteem.

9.1 Feeding Their Senses

If we think of all the ways we receive information our five senses are the channels through which we engage in the environment around us. Developing an approach to instil a sense of love through these channels can help to create a space in which children aren't just told they are loved, but they see, hear and feel it. These are some ways we can experience love through those lenses.

- **Touch:** Physical contact absolutely must feature at the top of this list for me, because it is an area in the care space which still faces challenges and confusion. There have been examples in the past of foster parents being trained to only provide a sideways hug. Physical affection should be appropriate and never forced. Offering a hug when a child is upset can be comforting and affirming. There have been numerous studies that show the severe and detrimental impact a lack of healthy affection can have on a child. I couldn't cover this point without drawing out why there is so much resistance to encouraging physical contact with care children. Many of them will have previously experienced either a lack of physical contact or unwanted physical contact or sexual abuse. These prior experiences can increase the risk of damage in these spaces, creating additional challenges to building a healthy foundation. There is a concern that foster carers will be accused of abusive contact, and some are counselled to maintain their distance in a way to mitigate the risk of a false allegation. There is also a suggestion that these low or no contact boundaries are there to protect the child.

I would suggest it does not reduce the likelihood of someone who wants to harm a child doing so. It does not mitigate the risk of a child making an unfounded allegation of abuse. It does reduce the possibility a child could misinterpret what is a healthy parental action as abusive. Though I wonder if a child does not learn from a foster parent what loving contact feels like, where will they learn it from? For me I was often left wondering what was wrong with me when I didn't get a response in a way I hoped. This could have even been just wanting a hug from a social worker. I only learnt what abusive love felt like. Of course I could see examples of what loving contact looked like between my foster parents or them and their children, but I lost something in never really learning how it felt.

- **Smell:** When mum passed away my siblings and I went to sort through her things. The only belonging I wanted to keep was a top she wore. It was not because of the design or the value. It was the smell. That top had somehow absorbed mum. I remember the days which followed. I would return to that top and try to breathe in that memory in the hope it would stick. For a child in care a sense of smell can be comforting, especially but not only for younger children. Keeping a blanket from home and not washing it when they first arrive. Cooking their favourite meal. Giving them something in their room which smells like home can all help build that sense of comfort and love.
- **Taste:** We all know children, and adults for that matter, who struggle to eat a varied and healthy diet. As a child in care I was certainly introduced to a much greater variety of food than I had ever experienced before. One of my foster mother's favourites was stuffed peppers. My foster sister and I hated them. We were told we had to

eat what we were given for tea. Sometimes the bin would even be checked to make sure we had not discarded the food. Whenever it was a stuffed pepper night we would linger at the table until everyone was out of earshot. Then we would take our peppers and walk all the way to the end of the long narrow garden before throwing them as far as we could over the neighbours' fences. We would rather go hungry that night. It is great to try to widen the palate of a child in your care and to aim to provide a healthy balanced diet. I would suggest it is also an act of love to ensure they have food they know and enjoy. Especially perhaps in those moments they are struggling or maybe when they first arrive. You can ask them what they like to eat or take them shopping with you. And when there is a celebration food is a great way to show your love and care.

- **Seeing:** My foster parents were not overly affectionate with each other, but thankfully they were not violent or abusive towards each other like my parents had been. There was the occasional argument in the house as there normally is, but these were infrequent and short lived. I did get to see the apologies they made to each other at times. I was grateful for the little examples of affection they showed. Modelling a healthy relationship is so important. We often learn best through examples and practice. If you do not feel there is that example in a child's life, simply talking about examples on the TV or their wider relationships and empathising the right and wrong behaviours is helpful.

- **Hearing:** Making sure the child hears positive things from you, social workers and teachers is extremely important. Repeat positive feedback or compliments. Be mindful if these are distressing for the child. If needed help them find support working towards a healthy acceptance of compliments, don't just stop offering them permanently. From a kind word to a completed homework assignment, every child achieves something worthy of praise each day. If you can't find one thing create an opportunity for them to achieve something small. To this day compliments are harder for me to hear than insults. That inner voice will tell me not to be stupid, don't buy it, you are a waste of space, they just pity you... The list goes on. My poor husband will be met with a quizzical, "Really?" when he says he loves me or pays me a compliment. I am grateful he has never stopped offering them even if I struggle to believe them. Every now and again when someone says something kind it breaks through the noise in my head. In those moments I feel a spark of something electric.

9.2 Unconditional Positive Regard

Beyond actions we can take to instil a sense of love in the world around them, building a solid foundation of unconditional positive regard is essential. The children you care for will all be different. Perhaps given their experiences in life that difference will feel more pronounced at times. Being mindful of their unique journey, trying not to make assumptions and creating a safe space where they can be themselves is vital. If you need help understanding who a child is, look for support from your wider network. If you suspect a child may be struggling with an aspect of their identity help them explore this, and ensure you respect anything you discover. Accept whatever behaviour a child may display. Consider that any perceived flaw can be reframed as a positive. Stubborn can be reframed as tenacious or headstrong as independent. Provide complete support and acceptance of them no matter what. The core foundation of a caring relationship is this unconditional positive regard. To build this sense of acceptance it can help to consider the following.

- **Focus on the child's strengths:** Celebrate their achievements, talents and positive qualities. Offer specific praise instead of generic compliments. When I was in care the school was an established source of strength focused development. I got to explore and concentrate on the things I was good at. I had wonderful teachers who helped me navigate the complex world of learning. They always highlighted the areas I could excel in. Even my English teacher who identified my dyslexia did it in an amazing way. She focused the discussion and tests almost entirely on the strength of my creative writing.

In every area of life – sports, business, happiness, there is one common lesson. No one becomes their best selves focusing on their weaknesses. Encourage the child to do enough to minimise the impact of those things which may hold them back, and focus the majority of their efforts on that one thing they are good at. With the aim they become great at it. Helping a child identify their thing and empowering them to focus their energy there can establish a path of success in later life.

- **Accept them for who they are:** Don't try to change them into someone they're not. Love them with their flaws and imperfections. My flaws included being stubborn beyond measure. I blame my nan and aunt for that wonderful trait. They certainly were strong examples of women who held high expectations and always stuck with their beliefs. Whilst that trait was a challenge at times for those caring for me, I also remember the moments of tender affection for this most ingrained part of my being. People would softly shake their heads, smile and say "You are stubborn Row." Those little moments of acceptance of who I was made me feel better about all the parts of myself.

The hardest part of me to accept in care was my sexuality and to some extent my gender identity. Back then I didn't know the term non-binary and yet there were lots of ways I didn't conform with the standard gender roles. I wanted to play rugby, and when on outdoor adventures with cadets I would be off with the boys. There was some level of acceptance that I was a little bit of a tomboy at times, but for my sexuality there was none. I never told my foster parents I was bisexual. There were clear examples of homophobia in the house. Not that it was a constant thing but the underhand remarks about someone else being a poof or "it" being wrong were woven through the subtext. I hid the fact that my first relationship was with a girl, and when I found myself for a few years with a guy I chose to ignore that part of me. Whether it is sexuality, religion or simply an unusual hobby, accepting a child wholly for who they are teaches them to be accepting of themselves.

9.3 Self-Care and Compassion

Self-care is an increasingly essential practice in our lives and a way we can demonstrate a love for ourselves in the moments we need it most. As we juggle more complexity, change and uncertainty there is more pressure to deliver, fit in, stand out and succeed. Many children in care will have had no opportunity to practice self-care. For many children who have had to focus on survival the idea of demonstrating that kindness towards themselves feels like an indulgence rather than essential. Here are some ways to help them establish good practices for self-care and compassion.

- **Self-acceptance and positive self-talk:** I previously mentioned positive self-talk and the power this can have in shifting a mindset. It is equally important to help children recognise that nobody is perfect. Either physically, emotionally, or in our actions we all get it wrong at times. In our house we have adopted the circle of trust. The children can come to us at any time and evoke the circle of trust. We hold hands and both have to say an age appropriate 'naughty word' then anything they tell us after that they cannot get in trouble for. Our girls have evoked it with anything from spilling a glass of milk to lying about where they went with a friend. It has been a great tool for talking through the mistake and supporting them to figure out by themselves how to fix it.

- **Cultivate self-compassion:** I am still trying to master this skill. I am finding more ways to demonstrate a little compassion towards myself from sitting down quietly for five minutes if I have a bad head, to taking an evening to binge watch telly if I can't the motivation to write. Encouraging a child to complete little acts of kindness towards themselves is a great way to build this foundation. If they are struggling to consider what to do to show themselves kindness it can help to reframe it and ask what would you say to or do for a friend if they were in your situation?

- **Establish Healthy Boundaries:** It is important to teach a child what healthy boundaries look and feel like. When they should establish these and how to maintain them. Identify opportunities where they can talk about and frame their decision within the context of a boundary. Be it a boundary on how they spend their time, who they engage with, the behaviour they will accept.

Boundaries and protecting your feelings and worth is a skill many children coming into care lack.

- **Practice self-care:** Throughout my time in care there was very little focus on establishing healthy habits. We had a fairly solid routine, a set bedtime etcetera, but the driver was never about educating us on the importance of these things. I left care with very little understanding of things like how a lack of sleep could impact my well-being, or the physical impact of a poor diet. Helping a child to learn about and establish healthy self-care practices can include discussions around the topic, practical assistance such as encouraging them to cook meals, or role modelling the right practices.

9.4 Summary.

Love or affection cannot be forced. Not every child has the expectation or desire to feel loved. They may just want to feel safe or understood. Showing love or kindness takes consideration and a little bit of trial and error. It does not have to be in the big gestures. Sometimes the greatest kindness is found in those small moments we show care. Changing the bedsheets, helping with homework, giving a little of your time. There will be setbacks but celebrate the progress you make together. Perhaps in time a sense of love will grow. Whether that feeling does or does not develop, instilling a sense of self-care in a child is a valuable way of helping them build a practice of compassion for themselves. It took me years to nurture that sense of kindness towards myself. For the longest time I would not even meet my bare essentials. I wouldn't take five minutes to sit quietly with a headache or make the children wait for food whilst I ran to the toilet. I was a master of deprioritising my needs. Having built a practice of self-care which allows me to sometimes decide to put my needs ahead of others, I recognise how much that enables me to give more. I have more patience, understanding and kindness towards others now I can practice it for myself.

CHAPTER 10

Thank You

I would not be here today if it was not for foster care. I wouldn't have this wonderful home, an amazing little family of my own, a husband I adore, an extra sister I admire, a job that I love. I wouldn't be alive if it was not for the kindness and courage of a stranger opening up their home. In doing so they gave me the chance of a future. I am so grateful for the people who have played a role in shaping the life I have. For the foster parents, foster brothers and sisters, teachers, social workers, bosses, friends and therapists. When in those quiet moments of a day I find myself reflecting on the wonder of my life, I think of them. I wonder if they realise how much of an impact they had.

When I left foster care I had been with my foster family for years. I loved them and the life I was living, but I had started to pull away from them. Perhaps because I could sense the end. I felt I needed to detach myself from that happiness before it was ripped away. The day I left was not planned. My sister had already been sent back to live with my father and his new fiancé.

I was visiting for her birthday. My father was drunk as he often was. He became aggressive and violent. The next day I decided I couldn't leave her. I went back to my foster parents, packed all my things in black bags and insisted I was leaving. I don't remember anyone asking why. Social services came and after a short discussion with my father my time in care was over.

It must have felt like a real blow for my foster parents. I know now from the foster parents I speak with they are often confused if a placement breaks down. Especially when they tried everything to show them care. The end of a fostering relationship is not the only challenge you are likely to face as a foster parent. Caring for these vulnerable children who are still sometimes embroiled in a world of turmoil, or at least carry the scars of the past, is a difficult thing. Caring for a foster child can be hard. Caring and looking after yourself is more important than ever in those moments when you find things are getting tough. Here are some of the ways you take care of yourself.

10.1 Acknowledging the Emotional Journey

Caring for a child in any circumstances comes with a myriad of highs and lows. The joys of seeing them grow and succeed. The frustration of repeating the same lessons over and over. The hurt when they say things which cut you to your core. The elation of seeing them happy. With many children in care the highs will be that much higher and the lows that much darker. Here are some ways you can recognise that you have your own emotional journey to travel on and support yourself through that process.

- **It is hard to say goodbye:** It is normal to feel sad, frustrated or confused when a placement ends, even if it's for the best. Try to prepare yourself for these big events. Perhaps consider keeping a carers journal, where you can collect photos and memories of the children you care for. You can ask the foster children to contribute to it occasionally and then you will have a keepsake you can look back on.

- **Let yourself grieve:** Allow yourself the space and time to grieve the loss of a relationship with a foster child and acknowledge your emotional investment. A lot of effort can go into supporting and caring for a foster child. Sometimes you may not notice the impact until it is over.

- **Be open:** It is important to create a safe space where you are able to express your feelings and concerns without judgement. That might be with a group of friends or a network of professionals. Make sure you have at least one person you can open up to if you are finding it hard.

10.2 Strategies for Fostering Resilience

Resilience is often thought of as our ability to take knocks, to work through the hard stuff and keep on going. There is that element to it. Some people might think of it as an ability to let stuff bounce off you. I believe there are two other aspects of resilience which are often overlooked. The ability to stretch yourself and the ability to recover. I think of it like an elastic band which is being pulled. The further you can stretch without snapping and the quicker you flex back to your norm, the more resilient you are. The strategies I have found to nurture my own resilience broadly fall into two categories. Firstly, proactive actions which need to be deployed or maintained before the challenge arises. The second can apply in the moment when you are faced with the difficult situation. As a foster parent or a professional caring for a child in care, one thing is for sure. You will need to nurture your levels of resilience. Here are some ideas to help you improve that elasticity.

- **Set boundaries:** As someone who works in the care of others it is really important to set healthy boundaries and maintain a personal life. None of us can pour from an empty cup, and sometimes the focus on the child can feel all consuming. You will have the best outcome for everyone if you maintain a level of commitment to your own life and happiness. This might mean trying to work appointments around your existing commitments or creating time in the evening when you can relax. These things often sound simple but can be hard to maintain. Perhaps considering prioritising the child's and your commitments so you know in advance that a visit to family for the child would trump a session at the gym, but an appointment with the social worker (which can be rearranged) would not trump your weekly yoga session. Everyone's priorities will be different. Proactively reflecting on what matters most can help you make the right decisions in the moment.

- **Maintain support networks:** Often we feel we need to hold things together ourselves. We decide that building a support network will create more effort than it is worth. That another link in the chain is a potential unknown, something which could go wrong rather than help. If we learn to recognise value in creating a varied multi strand approach to support, we can create a network which is robust and beneficial.

This can look like building multiple supports across a varied set of people. Don't become reliant on any one area or person. Consider support networks within the fostering space, within your personal or professional life. Build contacts and avenues for help in supporting your mental wellbeing. Understanding these ahead of time can allow you to tap into their support when you need it.

- **Focus on self-compassion:** With the complexities and challenges in caring for children we all at times will get it wrong. We may cause upset unintentionally or as a result of protecting the child or building a healthy boundary. It is easy to focus on these impacts and lose sight of all the successes. Practising self-compassion, acknowledging your efforts and celebrating your successes can help ensure you keep a focus on those areas you do succeed in. If it is feeling like an especially difficult time, set yourself realistic expectations and acknowledge when you achieve them. Or practice positivity fishing: at the end of your day reflect on all the moments which got you to that point in time and specifically search for all the positive points, things you achieved in the day no matter how big or small.

10.3 Taking Care of Yourself

There was a time in my life when I lived for our children or work. Honestly, I am not even sure my husband got much of a look in. I would spend most of my days working or with the kids and my evenings studying or working some more. Even now I have to make a conscious effort to create space for myself and my needs. When things get tricky it is even easier to let that focus slip and find myself only living for everyone around me. The greatest boundaries we can create other than in managing healthy relationships are the boundaries we place on our time.

- **Prioritise your physical health:** Healthy habits like regular exercise, balanced meals and sufficient sleep are a foundation on which most other things are built. Ensuring you have quick access to healthy options and considering meal preparation may improve your ability to stick with a healthy diet. Investing in sleep aids such as weighted blankets or daylight alarm clocks may assist with quality sleep. The most impactful action I have found with sleep is keeping to a consistent bedtime and wake time with a solid wind down routine. Consider including the family in opportunities to exercise. This can have the added benefit of teaching great behaviours, spending time together and supporting your fitness needs.

- **Engage in stress-relieving activities:** Many of us have heard of or attempted meditation. I would guess if you asked a random group of one hundred people if they meditated regularly, you could count the number on one hand. More recently the concept of a state of flow is becoming popular. This means taking the time to engage in an activity which allows us to effectively switch off. Finding this state of flow will vary for everyone. Perhaps your focused but relaxing state is when you go for a walk in nature, maybe it is when you are up to your elbows in grease working on a car, baking a cake or going for a drive. The idea is to find a low-level mental activity which requires little thinking but is enough to help you let go of any worries and be in the moment.

- **Seek professional help:** Many of us resist the idea of professional therapy. In the fostering space there can be a worry that admitting you need help will create problems in a professional context. I have known examples of people with diagnosed mental health conditions preventing them from becoming a foster parent. I have also seen examples where people with mental health conditions have gone on to be very successful foster parents. Sometimes we try to convince ourselves that our problems don't warrant help and others need it more. It is important to seek support if you are struggling to cope with the emotional demands of fostering.

10.4 Resilience in the Moment

You have done all the groundwork, established your healthy routines and support network. You still find yourself met with a situation you never expected, something which throws everything off kilter or creates a sense of chaos, worry or stress. I could probably write a whole book on this topic alone. Having been faced with hundreds of situations in my life which came close to breaking me but I worked through, I have certainly mastered many skills and strategies to help me through those minutes and into the next day. These are the ones I rely on most.

- **Breathe:** Breathing is often the first thing we lose control of in a difficult situation. Whether we find ourselves shortening each breath or taking one of those huge inhales which we then hold for eternity, noticing when your breath is altered can help you clock the first warning signs you are not coping. Then bringing control back to your breathing can provide immediate relief. Many people benefit from box breathing, inhaling for four and breathing out for four as you imagine drawing the sides of a box. The most effective form I have found is simply taking ten deep long breaths in and out. The importance is to feel the air sink deep into your stomach and to try and exhale for a longer period of time than the inhale. This can help to engage the parasympathetic nervous system and get yourself out of fight or flight.

- **Perspective:** In those moments we can't sit with the situation in front of us it can help to draw on a wider perspective. This might mean speaking to someone else or simply thinking about the situation within the context of your day, your week, your month or year. When we take a step back from them most issues can be recognised for the limited impact they will have over a lifetime.

- **Movement:** There is a reason we often see people who are stressed out depicted as pacing back and forth. The energy our bodies create when under stress needs to go somewhere. One of the best forms of stress relieving movement I have found in addition to exercise is to simply dance. Pop some music on and find yourself lost in the movement until you can work it out.

10.5 Thank You

These are just some of my reflections in the hope that you can create a little time to think about yourself and your needs. Caring for a child in the fostering system I hope provides more joy and opportunity than challenge. For me there is no greater act of kindness or charity than opening up your home and lives to a child in need. I didn't stay in contact with my foster parents when I left care, I didn't say thank you. I didn't get to tell them how grateful I was. So now in a life which is a sharp and glorious contrast to the one I knew, with a future I once couldn't even dream was possible, I get that chance to tell them how grateful I am.

For all the foster parents and people who care for us... Thank you. Thank you for the times you told me I could achieve something when I didn't believe it myself. Thank you for creating a safe space I could grow up in. Thank you for being the perfectly imperfect people you were. For showing me the kindness of the world I never knew existed. Thank you for giving me the joy of siblings. Thank you for giving me a space where I could just be me. Thank you for the lessons and for the advice. I know it wasn't always easy caring for me. I resisted your kindness and threw up all sorts of barriers you had to overcome. I know it was hard to watch me struggle. To listen to the experiences I had faced. To watch me try and fail and try again. In the quiet of my grateful heart, amidst the echoes of a challenging yet enriching journey, I hold onto this truth: foster care didn't just save my life – it gave me a family, a future, and the boundless gift of possibility. For all those who opened their hearts and homes, thank you for lighting my path with kindness and showing me the limitless power of compassion. Though you may never fully grasp the profound impact of your courage, compassion, and connection, know that it has written a future once only dreamed of.

Rowan Aderyn is an award-winning change maker, storyteller, and poet from Wales, whose journey from a traumatic childhood, marked by years of abuse and foster care, to a thriving career and life of advocacy is nothing short of inspiring. With a focus on mental health, gender, and inclusion, Rowan has channelled their experiences into founding a charity that supports those who have been through the care system. Their writing, celebrated for its lyrical beauty and emotional depth, delves into themes of love, trauma, and identity, with the aim of empowering others who have faced similar challenges and fostering greater understanding. Married for over fifteen years and a dedicated parent of two, Rowan continues to inspire and uplift through both their advocacy work and the powerful narratives they craft.